Sharon D. Williams
Alexander Garcia

Quantum worlds: The computing revolution and how it is shaping our future

bup

Sharon D. Williams
Alexander Garcia

Quantum worlds: The computing revolution and how it is shaping our future

ISBN: 978-3-68904-355-1 (Paperback)
ISBN: 978-3-68904-362-9 (e-book)

First edition
April 2024
Version 1.0
Printed in the European Union
bup@bremenuniversitypress.com
www.bremenuniversitypress.com

Sharon D. Williams
Alexander Garcia

Quantum worlds: The computing revolution and how it is shaping our future

Overview

Table of contents

AREAS OF APPLICATION FOR QUANTUM COMPUTERS 95

THE FUTURE OF QUANTUM COMPUTERS 107

Introduction

Quantum computers are on everyone's lips for several reasons.

They represent a significant advance in the way we think about data processing and computer technology and promise breakthroughs in many scientific and industrial fields. They are also - unlike in the past - no longer just the domain of highly specialised researchers and scientists. In view of the expected applications, which could have a massive impact on many areas of everyone's life, it is time to write a generally understandable work on this subject. Quantum computers concern us all.

One of the main reasons for the high level of interest in quantum computers is their theoretical ability to solve problems that are practically unsolvable for conventional computers. This includes complex simulations in physics, chemistry and materials science, the improvement of algorithms for artificial intelligence, the optimisation of large systems, for example in logistics or financial models, and not least the possibility of breaking existing encryption techniques. The ability to discover and develop new drugs more quickly by simulating molecular interactions more precisely is another example of the enormous potential of quantum computers.

Finally, the basis of quantum computers - quantum mechanics - is fascinating due to its non-intuitiveness and its challenge to our understanding of the laws of nature. Quantum mechanics, one of the pillars of modern physics, contradicts many aspects of descriptive classical physics, which leads to a mixture of fascination and alienation. The application of its principles in a technology that has the potential to change our society therefore arouses the interest not only of experts, but also of the general public.

All in all, it is the ground-breaking possibilities, the technological challenges and the profound scientific questions that make quantum computers such a centre of interest.

The idea that quantum computers are already capable of performing computing operations that would take the most powerful conventional computer thousands of years marks a turning point in the world of information processing. This performance advantage, which the first quantum computers have already demonstrated in specialised tasks, underlines the transformative potential of quantum technology. It is a clear signal that we are at the beginning of a ground-breaking development that brings with it both immense opportunities and significant challenges.

The exemplary scenario, in which a quantum computer solves a task in minutes that would take a classical supercomputer thousands of years, illustrates the unique ability of quantum computers to tackle problems by exploiting quantum phenomena such as superposition and entanglement in a way that is unimaginable in the

5

classical world. This capability has the potential to revolutionise research in fields such as materials science, drug discovery, artificial intelligence and many others by offering completely new possibilities for modelling complex systems and solving optimisation problems.

At the same time, the ongoing development of quantum computers raises important questions about the security of existing cryptographic systems, which form the backbone of digital security worldwide. The possibility of compromising established encryption methods requires a proactive revision of security protocols and the development of new cryptographic approaches that are resistant to quantum attacks.

Addressing the topic of quantum computing is therefore not only important for scientists, technologists and industry players, but also for politicians, security experts and ultimately for society as a whole. Education and public awareness play an important role in understanding the opportunities and risks associated with this technology and making informed decisions about its development and application.

We are at the beginning of an era in which quantum technologies have the potential to fundamentally change our world. It is crucial that we embark on this journey with a deep understanding of the technology itself and a clear view of its potential impact. The development and implementation of quantum technologies has required careful consideration of the ethical, societal and safety aspects to ensure that this revolutionary technology is used for the benefit of humanity.

Quantum computers represent a revolutionary way of processing information that differs fundamentally from classical computers. Their concept is based on the principles of quantum mechanics, a theory that describes the behaviour of matter and energy on the smallest scales of the universe. Unlike classical computers, which process data in the form of bits that can assume either the state 0 or 1, quantum computers utilise quantum bits or qubits. A qubit can exist not only in the states 0 or 1, but also in superpositions of both, known as superposition. This ability allows quantum computers to represent and process an enormous number of possible states simultaneously.

Another fundamental principle of quantum computing is entanglement, a phenomenon in which qubits are linked together in a state so that the state of a single qubit can immediately influence the state of another, regardless of the distance between them. This enables a type of parallel processing that is unattainable in classical systems.

These properties mean that quantum computers can potentially perform certain types of calculations much faster than their classical counterparts, particularly those involving the factorisation of large numbers, the simulation of quantum systems and certain optimisation problems.

However, the challenges of building and scaling quantum computers are considerable. Qubits are extremely susceptible to external disturbances, a phenomenon known as decoherence, which can destroy their quantum states. Therefore, quantum computers require extremely low temperatures and special shielding to be operational. Despite these challenges, researchers are making steady progress and there are already working quantum computers with a limited number of qubits that are used for specialised research tasks and experimental applications.

Developments in the field of quantum computing could have a huge impact on numerous fields in the long term, from materials science to pharmacy and cryptography. The ability to solve problems that are practically unsolvable for conventional computers opens up new horizons in science and technology. However, there is still a lot of research and development work to be done before quantum computers are ready for widespread use.

Quantum computers represent a fundamental departure from traditional computing technologies by utilising principles of quantum mechanics to perform data processing tasks that are either very time-consuming or practically impossible for classical computers. This new type of computer uses quantum bits, or qubits, instead of classical bits to store and process information.

We take you on a journey through the exciting history and future of quantum computers, which will soon define all our lives in ways that can only be guessed at today.

Basic concepts

Quantum bits (qubits)

At the heart of a quantum computer lie qubits. Unlike classical bits, which exist in one of two possible states, 0 or 1, qubits can be in a state that is a superposition of both 0 and 1 thanks to the principle of superposition. This ability allows qubits to carry and process more information than classical bits.

Superposition is a state that qubits can be in, and it allows a qubit to hold different probabilities for the state 0 and 1 at the same time. When a system of N qubits is in superposition, it can represent 2^N different states simultaneously, which represents an exponential increase in information processing capacity compared to N classical bits.

Another phenomenon of quantum mechanics that is used in quantum computers is entanglement. Two or more qubits can exist in an entangled state, in which the state of a single qubit directly determines the state of the other qubits involved, regardless of their spatial distance. Entanglement enables complex coordination and simultaneous calculations that are unattainable in classical systems.

Quantum computers also utilise the phenomenon of quantum interference to control the probabilities of qubit states, thereby eliminating undesirable computational results while amplifying the desired results.

Functionality and challenges

Quantum computers perform computations by manipulating qubits and utilising the principles of superposition and entanglement to achieve enormous parallel processing capacity. Quantum algorithms specifically designed to utilise these properties can solve certain types of problems much more efficiently than the best known algorithms for classical computers.

One of the biggest technical obstacles to the development of quantum computers is decoherence, a process in which the sensitive quantum states of qubits are disturbed by their interaction with the environment, leading to a loss of quantum information. The realisation of reliable quantum error correction methods and the development of stable qubits that can remain in their quantum state for longer are key areas of research

Areas of application and potential

Quantum computers offer promising new possibilities in many areas.

They could challenge existing encryption systems and at the same time promote the development of new quantum encryption methods.

By simulating molecules and chemical reactions, quantum computers could make revolutionary progress in the discovery of new materials and medicines.

They could find more efficient solutions to complex optimisation problems in areas such as logistics, manufacturing and finance.

The future of quantum computers is extremely promising, but faces significant technical and theoretical challenges. Advances in quantum technology, the development of quantum algorithms and the overcoming of technical obstacles such as decoherence and error-proneness will be crucial to realise the full potential of quantum computers. In the long term, quantum computers could not only reshape existing computational paradigms, but also open up new avenues in research and enable previously unimaginable scientific breakthroughs.

A brief history of quantum computers

The history of quantum computing is both fascinating and complex, characterised by theoretical breakthroughs and experimental advances that together form the foundation of this revolutionary technology. Here is an overview of some of the most important milestones on the road to the development of quantum computers:

1980s: Theoretical foundations

In 1981, Richard Feynman proposed that quantum computers could be used to simulate physical systems that are too complex for classical computers. Feynman identified the inherent difficulty of simulating quantum systems using classical means and argued that a new approach based on quantum mechanics was necessary.

In 1982, Paul Benioff described the concept of a quantum Turing machine, the theoretical foundation for quantum computing, which shows that quantum systems could be used for calculations.

David Deutsch develops the idea further in 1985 and proposes the quantum Turing machine formalism, which lays the theoretical foundation for quantum computers. He also presents the concept of the universal quantum computer, which is capable of performing any computable function.

1990s: Breakthrough in quantum algorithms

In 1994, Peter Shor developed the Shor algorithm named after him, which shows that a quantum computer can factorise large numbers much more efficiently than the best known algorithms for classical computers. This breakthrough has significant implications for cryptography, in particular for the security of many encryption systems.

In 1996, Lov Grover developed the Grover algorithm, which performs a search in an unsorted database quadratically faster than any classical algorithm. This demonstrates the potential superiority of quantum computers for certain search tasks.

2000s: First quantum computers

In the early 2000s, researchers began to build the first quantum computers capable of executing simple quantum algorithms. These early systems are still a long way from practical applicability, but mark important technical milestones.

2010s: Approaching quantum superiority

In 2019, Google announced that its Sycamore quantum computer had achieved quantum supremacy by performing a specific calculation in 200 seconds that would take the world's most powerful supercomputer around 10,000 years. This milestone is seen as the beginning of a new era in quantum computing, although practical applications are still a long way off.

Future prospects

Today, research is primarily focussed on improving the stability and scalability of qubits, developing fault-tolerant quantum computers and finding practical applications for quantum technologies. The development from the first theoretical proposals to the demonstration of quantum superiority shows how far quantum computer technology has come. Future developments promise to be even more exciting, with the potential to profoundly change science, technology and society.

Basic principles of quantum computer technology

Quantum computing technology is based on the principles of quantum mechanics, a field of physics that describes the behaviour of particles on the smallest possible scale. This technology differs fundamentally from classical computer technology, which is based on bits that can assume either the state 0 or 1. At the centre of quantum computer technology are quantum bits or qubits, which enable much more complex data processing thanks to the principles of superposition and entanglement.

Superposition is the first key principle that enables qubits to be in a state that corresponds to a combination of 0 and 1. This allows a qubit to perform multiple calculations simultaneously. This parallel processing capability potentially significantly increases the computing speed and efficiency of quantum computers compared to classical computers for certain tasks.

The second key principle is entanglement, a phenomenon in which the state of one qubit is directly linked to the state of another qubit, regardless of the distance between them. This deep connection enables exceptionally coordinated data processing across multiple qubits. Entangled qubits can transmit information in a way that is not possible with classical communication, which is particularly valuable for applications in quantum cryptography and quantum networks.

Another important concept in quantum computing technology is quantum interference, which is used to superimpose the probabilities of qubit states in such a way that undesirable computational paths are cancelled while desirable paths are strengthened. This is crucial for developing efficient algorithms for quantum computers that can solve specific tasks, such as the factorisation of large numbers, a task where quantum computers have a theoretical advantage over classical computers.

Quantum error correction is another key consideration. Quantum states are highly susceptible to perturbations from their environment, a phenomenon known as "decoherence". The development of error-correcting codes that can preserve the integrity of quantum information in a noisy, decoherent environment is crucial for the practical use of quantum computers.

The challenges in realising practical quantum computing are enormous, including technical obstacles in producing and maintaining states required for quantum computation, as well as developing algorithms that specifically take advantage of quantum computing. Despite these challenges, research and development in quantum computing technology is moving forward, with significant advances in materials science, cryo-engineering, quantum algorithms and other areas that have the potential to push the boundaries of computability and information.

Qubits and their properties

The fascination with qubits, or quantum bits, stems from their ability to push the boundaries of classical computer technology by utilising the exotic principles of quantum mechanics. Unlike classical bits, which form the backbone of traditional computer technology and always assume one of two possible states, 0 or 1, qubits break this binary constraint and allow a much richer form of data processing.

A key aspect that makes qubits so special is their ability to superpose. This phenomenon allows a qubit to be in a state that is a superposition of both 0 and 1. Imagine that a classical bit could only be either red or green, while a qubit can be both red and green to varying degrees. This superposition exponentially expands the amount of information that a single qubit can hold compared to a classical bit, and allows a set of qubits to simultaneously represent a huge amount of different states.

Another remarkable feature of qubits is quantum entanglement, a state in which two or more qubits are connected in such a way that the state of a single qubit cannot be described independently of the states of the others. This invention allows information to be transferred between qubits even if they are spatially separated, which can lead to extremely efficient computational processes. Entangled qubits can act in a coordinated manner, even over large distances, without direct communication between them.

Superposition and entanglement together create the basis for the superior computational capabilities of quantum computers. These properties allow quantum computers to tackle complex problems in a way that is unattainable for classical computers. For example, they can solve certain mathematical problems, such as the factorisation of large numbers, much faster, which has important implications for cryptography. They could also revolutionise the development of new drugs by making it possible to simulate molecular interactions at a level that was previously inaccessible.

Despite its enormous potential, qubit technology is still in the early stages of development. The practical realisation of this technology faces considerable technical challenges, including increasing the stability of qubits and protecting them from external interference that could affect their sensitive quantum states.

Overlay

The ability of qubits to superimpose is a cornerstone that distinguishes quantum computer technology from classical computer technology and gives it extraordinary potential. Superposition enables qubits to be in a state that can be understood as a combination of the classical states 0 and 1. These states are described by quantum mechanics, with the amplitude of the states indicating the probability of finding the qubit in one of the two classical states during a measurement. The mathematical representation of such a state uses complex numbers to describe both the amplitude and the phase of these superpositions, resulting in a rich structure of information possibilities that goes far beyond what is possible with a simple bit.

Superposition allows quantum computers to work in parallel by exploring multiple computational paths simultaneously. Unlike a classical computer, which must sequentially traverse every possible path, a quantum computer with n qubits can theoretically explore up to 2^n states simultaneously. This parallel processing capacity is particularly useful for problems where a large number of possible solutions need to be searched through quickly, such as optimisation, factorisation of large numbers or search algorithms.

The exponential nature of information processing in quantum computers through superposition opens up revolutionary possibilities, but also poses practical challenges. In order to utilise this parallel processing power effectively, specific quantum algorithms must be developed that take into account the peculiarities of quantum mechanics. Probably the best-known quantum algorithm, Shor's algorithm for factorising large numbers, demonstrates the potential of quantum computers to solve certain problems much more efficiently than classical computers.

However, the realisation of these potentials is complex in practice. The superposition states are highly susceptible to external perturbations, leading to decoherence - the loss of the quantum mechanical states necessary for calculations. Developing robust quantum systems and maintaining coherence over time periods long enough for meaningful computations remains one of the biggest challenges in quantum computing technology.

Furthermore, utilising the parallel processing capacity provided by superposition requires the development of new programming paradigms and algorithms. Quantum programming is fundamentally different from classical programming as it directly utilises the unique properties of qubits, such as superposition and entanglement, to solve problems in new ways.

Entanglement

The entanglement of qubits epitomises one of the most difficult phenomena in quantum physics, which not only challenges our understanding of space and time, but also forms the basis for ground-breaking applications in quantum technology. Albert Einstein coined the term "spooky action at a distance" to express his scepticism and fascination with the idea that two or more particles can be connected in a way that appears to be independent of the distance between them. This property contradicted Einstein's idea of a local reality in which objects can only be influenced by direct interactions in their immediate surroundings.

In the world of quantum mechanics, entanglement allows the state of one qubit to affect the state of another qubit instantaneously, regardless of how far apart they are. This means that measurements on one qubit can have instantaneous effects on the state of an entangled qubit, even if they are light years apart. This non-local property has far-reaching implications and enables completely new approaches to information processing and transmission.

The applications of quantum entanglement in quantum computer technology and communication are diverse and revolutionary. In quantum cryptography, for example, entanglement enables extremely secure communication methods. By creating entangled qubit pairs, two parties can exchange an absolutely secure key, as any attempt to eavesdrop would disrupt the entanglement and thus be detected immediately. This utilises the inherent uncertainty of quantum states to ensure the security of communication.

In quantum computing, entanglement makes it possible to perform complex calculations in a way that is not possible with classical computers. By designing algorithms that operate on entangled qubits, quantum computers can potentially perform tasks such as simulating molecules or cracking encryption, which would overwhelm classical computers, in a drastically reduced time.

Despite the enormous potential, the practical realisation and maintenance of entangled states in quantum systems represents a major challenge. The generation and manipulation of entangled qubits requires extremely precise control and shielding from any form of environmental influences that could disturb the sensitive quantum states. Research and development in this area is intensive and aims to develop robust quantum systems that can fully realise the promise of quantum entanglement.

Basics of entanglement

The apparent discrepancy between quantum entanglement and the theory of relativity has led to discussions and investigations in physics. The theory of relativity, formulated by Albert Einstein, states that no information or effect can travel faster than light. At first glance, quantum entanglement, in which the measurement of one qubit instantly determines the state of another, spatially separated qubit, might appear to violate this principle. The key to understanding why this is not a contradiction lies in the type of information transmitted and the nature of entanglement itself.

No conventional information or signals are transferred between the qubits during entanglement. Instead, a correlation is established that only becomes apparent when measurements are made and compared. So when you measure an entangled pair of qubits, the measurement of one qubit instantaneously determines the state of the other, but this change cannot be used to transmit information at faster-than-light speeds. This means that entanglement does not violate the causal structure of spacetime as described by the theory of relativity.

The correlation between entangled qubits is a result of their common history and the quantum mechanical laws that govern them, not a transfer of information in the classical sense. This phenomenon demonstrates the non-locality of quantum mechanics, which states that parts of an entangled system cannot be considered completely independent of each other, regardless of their spatial distance. However, this non-locality does not constitute a mechanism for the instantaneous transmission of recognisable information, thereby preserving the integrity of the theory of relativity.

Quantum entanglement and its apparent instantaneity therefore do not contradict the limited transmission speed of information according to the theory of relativity. Instead, they force us to rethink our notions of causality and separation in a universe that is profoundly characterised by quantum properties. This finely tuned interplay between quantum mechanics and relativity remains a fascinating field for theoretical and experimental research that continues to expand our understanding of the fundamental principles of the universe.

Applications of entanglement

The unique properties of entanglement have many applications in quantum information theory and technology.

Quantum cryptography

The BB84 protocol, which was introduced by Charles Bennett and Gilles Brassard in 1984, is a milestone in quantum cryptography and marks the beginning of a new era in secure communication.

Although the BB84 protocol itself is not directly based on quantum entanglement, but on the principles of quantum mechanics, in particular indeterminacy, there are related protocols that utilise entanglement to further enhance security. The fundamental principle behind BB84 and related protocols is the use of unique quantum properties to generate and verify a secure key, which can then be used to encrypt messages.

In the BB84 protocol, the sender, often called Alice, sends a series of qubits to the receiver, Bob, with each qubit in one of four possible states. These states represent two different bases (for example, the polarisation of photons), and the qubits are sent in a randomly selected base. Bob also measures each incoming qubit in a randomly selected base. After all qubits have been transmitted, Alice and Bob publicly share the bases in which they were sent and measured, respectively, without revealing the results of the measurements. Qubits where the bases match are used to generate the key, while the others are discarded.

The security of the protocol is based on two important quantum principles. Firstly, Heisenberg's uncertainty principle states that the measurement process of a quantum state inevitably disturbs it if the state is not measured in the correct basis. Secondly, the no-cloning theorem of quantum mechanics prohibits the creation of exact copies of unknown quantum states. These properties ensure that any attempt by an eavesdropper to eavesdrop on the key exchange will inevitably leave a trace by influencing Alice and Bob's measurement results. By comparing a subset of their measurement results, Alice and Bob can determine whether security is guaranteed. If the error rate is below a certain threshold, they can assume that the exchange was secure; otherwise, they must assume that the key has been compromised and the process must be repeated.

While BB84 and its derivatives already provide a high level of security, protocols based on quantum entanglement, such as the Ekert protocol (E91), extend the security features by utilising entangled qubit pairs. Here, any attempt to eavesdrop not only results in a disturbance that can be detected, but the entanglement itself provides an even stronger basis for security as the correlations between entangled qubits are used for key generation and verification.

These advances in quantum cryptography promise almost unbreakable security, as they are based on the fundamental laws of physics and not just the complexity of mathematical problems. The continued development and implementation of these technologies could fundamentally change the future of secure communication.

Quantum computing

Entanglement plays a central role in the extraordinary performance of quantum computers by enabling states and operations to be coordinated across multiple qubits, leading to an exponential increase in information processing capacity over classical computers. This capability is particularly important for the implementation of advanced quantum algorithms, such as Shor's algorithm for factoring large numbers and Grover's algorithm for efficiently searching databases.

Shor's algorithm is perhaps the best-known example of the superiority of quantum computers for specific tasks. Traditional algorithms for factorising large numbers, a task that is critical to the security of many of today's cryptographic systems, require exponentially more computing time as the size of the numbers increases. However, Shor's quantum algorithm can factorise these numbers in polynomial time, meaning that it requires only moderately more computing resources as the number length increases. This efficiency gain could theoretically compromise the security of most current encryption systems, as they are based on the difficulty of factorising large numbers.

Grover's algorithm, on the other hand, offers a quadratic speed advantage for searching in unsorted databases. While a classic algorithm has to search through half of all entries on average before it finds the desired entry, Grover's algorithm reduces the number of necessary search steps to the square root of the total number of entries. This means that for a database with one million entries, only about 1,000 search operations are needed instead of 500,000. Although this advantage is not as dramatic as that of Shor's algorithm for factorisation, it could have a significant impact for certain applications, such as in cryptography and in solving certain optimisation problems.

Implementing these algorithms on a quantum computer requires careful control of entanglement between qubits. Entanglement allows qubits to interact in a coherent state, which is necessary for parallel execution of computations across exponentially many states. This parallel processing capability is the key to the superiority of quantum computers in certain tasks.

Despite the impressive potential of these algorithms, the practical challenges of realising powerful quantum computers are considerable. These include generating and maintaining entanglement over a large number of qubits, minimising errors through quantum decoherence and the general problem of scalability of quantum systems. However, research in these areas is very active and progress in the development of error correction mechanisms and the production of more stable qubits gives hope that quantum computers that can use these algorithms effectively will be realised in the future.

Quantum teleportation

Quantum teleportation is a fascinating phenomenon that results directly from the unique properties of quantum entanglement and has the potential to fundamentally change the way information is transmitted. At its core, quantum teleportation allows the quantum state of one qubit to be transferred to another qubit over arbitrary distances without the need for physical transfer of the qubit itself or its individual properties. This concept may sound like science fiction at first, but it is based on solid physical principles and has already been demonstrated experimentally.

The quantum teleportation procedure begins with a pair of entangled qubits that are split between two parties, often called Alice and Bob. Alice has another qubit whose state she wants to transfer to Bob. To perform the teleportation, Alice performs a special measurement on her qubit and her part of the entangled pair. This

28

measurement changes the state of her entangled qubit in a way that depends on the state of the qubit to be teleported, even though these two qubits have never directly interacted with each other.

The crucial element here is that Alice's measurement also influences the state of Bob's qubit, thanks to the magical connection created by the entanglement. However, at this point Bob does not yet know what state his qubit is in. In order to accurately reconstruct the original state of Alice's qubit, Alice must communicate the result of her measurement to him via a classical communication channel. With this information, Bob can then perform a series of operations on his qubit to reconstruct the exact state of Alice's original qubit.

It is important to emphasise that no information is transmitted faster than light in quantum teleportation. The need to transmit the result of the measurement via a classical channel ensures that quantum teleportation does not violate the theory of relativity. Furthermore, no matter or energy is transmitted in the strict sense; instead, the state of a qubit is transmitted, which is a more subtle form of information transfer.

Quantum teleportation has important implications for the development of quantum networks and quantum communication. It enables the secure transmission of quantum information over long distances and is a key concept for the realisation of quantum internet, where information is based on quantum states and can thus reach a new level of security and efficiency.

Furthermore, quantum teleportation could be used in future quantum computing systems to transfer quantum information between different parts of a quantum computer or even between different quantum computers, which could significantly advance the development of scalable quantum computing systems and complex quantum networks.

Problems of entanglement

The practical use of quantum entanglement still faces numerous challenges. The generation and maintenance of entangled states is technically demanding, as qubits are extremely susceptible to decoherence due to environmental influences. The development of technologies that enable stable entanglement states over longer periods of time and over greater distances is an active field of research.

Coherence and decoherence

The concepts of coherence and decoherence are central to the understanding and development of quantum computing technology. They concern the stability of quantum states, which are essential for the realisation of calculations in quantum computers.

Coherence

Coherence in the quantum world is a central concept that describes the fundamental ability of quantum systems to be in a well-defined state of superposition or entanglement and to maintain this state over time.

This ability is essential for the functioning of quantum computers, as it forms the basis for performing quantum computations. The coherence time defines the critical time window within which quantum information can be processed before unavoidable interactions with the environment - a process known as decoherence - disrupt the quantum states to such an extent that they lose their quantum mechanical properties.

Achieving longer coherence times is one of the most important research priorities in the development of quantum computers, as they directly influence the performance and practicability of these systems. The longer the coherence time of a qubit, the more operations can theoretically be performed on it before decoherence makes the calculations unreliable. This enables more complex algorithms and the solution of more demanding problems. To increase coherence times, scientists are exploring various approaches, such as improving the physical isolation of qubits, developing qubits that are less susceptible to environmental influences, and applying advanced error correction techniques that can compensate for the effects of decoherence.

Furthermore, coherence time is a crucial factor for the scalability of quantum computers. For practical applications, quantum systems must be able to process thousands or even millions of qubits while maintaining sufficient coherence time to perform meaningful computations. This requires advances not only in materials science and quantum technology, but also in theoretical physics and algorithmics to develop efficient methods to utilise and protect coherence in complex quantum systems.

Decoherence

Decoherence is one of the biggest obstacles to the development and scaling of quantum computers. It is a fundamental challenge as it directly affects the ability of quantum computers to store and process information. The process of decoherence causes the quantum states of qubits to "merge" with their environment, resulting in the loss of characteristic quantum properties such as superposition and entanglement. In practice, this means that qubits cannot maintain their state long enough to perform complex computations before degrading to a classical state in which they function like conventional bits.

The interactions that lead to decoherence can be diverse in nature, including thermal, electromagnetic and even cosmic influences. Any interaction with the external environment, no matter how small, can be enough to disrupt the fragile quantum superposition of a qubit. Therefore, maintaining quantum coherence requires extremely controlled environmental conditions, such as deep cold close to absolute zero and the use of shielding against electromagnetic radiation.

Research in the field of quantum computing technology is strongly focused on finding ways to minimise decoherence and extend the coherence times of qubits. One approach is to develop qubits that are inherently more resistant to decoherence. This includes, for example, topological qubits, which are based on the principles of topological quantum computing and are theoretically more stable against local disturbances. Another approach is the use of dynamic correction methods and error correction codes, which make it possible to recognise and correct errors caused by decoherence without measuring or disturbing the quantum information itself.

Control of decoherence

Controlling or minimising decoherence is a major technical challenge in quantum computing technology. Researchers and engineers are developing various strategies to extend the coherence times of qubits and minimise decoherence effects:

Isolation of qubits

Minimising interactions between qubits and their environment is crucial to delay decoherence and improve the performance of quantum computers. Various technological solutions and advanced techniques are applied to minimise the external perturbations that lead to decoherence. Here are some of the most important methods used in quantum computing technology:

- Vacuum chambers: Vacuum chambers play an important role in reducing decoherence by removing air and other gases that could interact with the qubits. By creating a nearly particle-free environment, the likelihood of collisions between the qubits and air molecules is reduced, resulting in a more stable quantum environment. This is particularly important for experiments and quantum computers that rely on systems such as ion trap-based qubits, where charged particles serve as qubits.
- Cryo-cooling: Cryo-cooling is another critical technology for delaying decoherence. Many quantum computing systems, especially those based on superconducting qubits, require extremely low temperatures, often only a few millikelvin above absolute zero. At these temperatures, almost all thermal activity is greatly reduced, minimising the interaction of the qubits with their environment and extending coherence times. Cryocooling also helps to reduce the thermal excitation of the qubits themselves, which is another potential source of decoherence.
- Shielding: Shielding against electromagnetic radiation is crucial to minimise external interference that could disturb the quantum states of the qubits. This includes protection from radio frequency radiation, magnetic fields and even cosmic rays. By using materials that absorb or reflect electromagnetic waves, researchers can preserve

the integrity of the quantum information in the qubits.

- In addition to physical shielding techniques, researchers are also developing advanced error correction codes and dynamic decoherence cancellation techniques. These methods aim to correct or compensate for the effects of decoherence even when it occurs. By applying complex algorithms, quantum computers can recognise and correct potential errors without destroying the quantum information itself.
- Development of new qubit systems: Finally, work is underway to develop new types of qubits that are naturally less susceptible to decoherence. This could reduce the need for extremely stringent environmental controls and facilitate the practical application of quantum computers.

These methods and technologies are important for advancing quantum computing technology and overcoming the challenges posed by decoherence. By continuously improving these techniques and developing new approaches to control the quantum environment, scientists are striving to push the boundaries of what is possible with quantum computers.

Error correction and error tolerance

The development of quantum error correction codes and fault-tolerant algorithms represents a decisive advance in quantum computer technology. These approaches enable quantum computers to perform correct calculations despite the inevitable decoherence and other sources of error. Quantum error correction codes work by distributing quantum information across multiple qubits so that even if some qubits are affected by decoherence or other perturbations, the original information can be reconstructed from the remaining error-free qubits.

- Quantum error correction: The basic idea of quantum error correction is similar to classical error correction, but is much more complex due to the quantum nature of the information - such as superposition and entanglement. Quantum error correction codes use entanglement to distribute quantum states across a group of qubits in such a way that errors affecting a single qubit or a small group of qubits can be detected and corrected without measuring the quantum information itself. This makes it possible to avoid the destructive effects of decoherence, as the information is not stored in the individual qubits but in their collective state.

- Fault-tolerant algorithms: Fault-tolerant quantum algorithms are those that are designed to work correctly even in the presence of errors caused by the imperfections of qubits and operations. These algorithms are designed to effectively utilise the corrections provided by error correction codes to ensure that the calculations produce reliable results.

- Resource requirements: The implementation of quantum error correction and fault-tolerant algorithms requires a significant increase in the number of qubits in a quantum computer. For every logical qubit used for computation, tens or even hundreds of physical qubits may be required to provide the necessary redundancy for effective error correction. This requirement poses a significant technical challenge, as it compounds the already existing difficulties of scaling quantum computing systems and maintaining coherence across large numbers of qubits.

Despite the challenges, quantum error correction and fault-tolerant algorithms offer a feasible way to enable reliable quantum computation and are thus an active area of research. Continuously improving qubit quality, increasing coherence times and developing more efficient error correction codes could help to reduce the required number of physical qubits and make feasible fault-tolerant quantum computers a reality.

Dynamic decoherence suppression

Dynamic Decoherence Suppression (DDS) represents an advanced strategy to combat decoherence in quantum systems. This technique involves the use of specially designed control sequences to minimise the negative effects of environmental perturbations on the coherence of qubits. DDS aims to actively extend the coherence times of qubits by cancelling out external and internal perturbations that lead to decoherence. This allows qubits to maintain their quantum mechanical states over longer periods of time, which is crucial for performing complex quantum computations.

- Basic principles of dynamic decoherence suppression: Dynamic decoherence suppression is based on the precise manipulation of qubits by a sequence of control pulses. These pulses are designed to detect and neutralise specific types of perturbations acting on a qubit. The control sequences act like a stabilisation system that protects the qubits from the "shocks" of the outside world.
- Implementation: The implementation of DDS requires a deep understanding of the specific mechanisms that lead to decoherence in a given quantum system. This includes knowledge of the types of perturbations, their frequencies and amplitudes. With this information, researchers can develop customised control sequences that specifically counteract these perturbations. The sequences can consist of a variety of physical operations, such as electromagnetic pulses, which are directed at the qubits to correct their states over time and keep them stable.

Although dynamic decoherence suppression is a promising approach, it also poses challenges. The development of effective control sequences requires a precise knowledge of the specific dynamics of the quantum system and the interactions with its environment. In addition, the control pulses must be applied with great precision to avoid unwanted perturbations that could introduce additional errors into the system. This requires sophisticated experimental techniques and the ability to manipulate quantum systems with extraordinary accuracy.

Despite the technical challenges, dynamic decoherence cancellation offers a promising way to improve the performance of quantum computers. By extending coherence times, it opens up the possibility of running more complex algorithms and pushing the boundaries of what can be achieved with quantum technology. Continued research and development in this area could lead to even more effective methods of decoherence suppression and make an important contribution to the realisation of practical quantum computers.

Significance for quantum computer technology

Ongoing research efforts in quantum computing technology are aimed at overcoming the challenges of coherence conservation and decoherence control to lay the foundation for practical quantum systems. The ability to keep quantum states stable over long periods of time is crucial as it directly influences the complexity and nature of the problems that can be solved with quantum computers. Advances in these areas could enable quantum computers to tackle tasks that are impractical or impossible for classical computers due to computational time or resource constraints.

- Materials science: A key aspect of the research focuses on the development of new materials and qubit designs that are inherently more resistant to environmental influences and thus enable longer coherence times. The discovery and application of materials that can operate at higher temperatures or under less restrictive conditions could significantly reduce the operating costs and complexity of quantum computing systems.
- Error correction and fault tolerance: The improvement and implementation of quantum error correction codes and fault-tolerant algorithms is another key area of research. These techniques make it possible to detect and correct errors caused by unavoidable decoherence processes, thereby increasing the reliability of quantum computations. The development of more efficient error correction methods could reduce the number of physical qubits required per logical qubit and improve the practicability of quantum computers.
- Control and shielding techniques: Research in advanced control and shielding techniques, including dynamic decoherence cancellation, aims to precisely control the interactions of qubits with their environment. By applying specific

pulse sequences and designing systems that are protected against external disturbances, scientists can minimise the effects of decoherence. The further development of these technologies promises a significant increase in coherence times.

- Scalability and system integration: In order to realise practically usable quantum systems, it is necessary to find solutions for scaling quantum computers that can efficiently integrate and manage a large number of qubits. This includes the development of architectures and technological platforms that enable reliable communication and interaction between qubits over long distances and in complex networks.

Realising these goals requires multidisciplinary collaboration between physicists, engineers, materials scientists and computer scientists. Ongoing progress in these fields promises not only the development of quantum computers that can solve complex problems efficiently, but also the opening up of new areas of research and applications in cryptography, materials science, chemical synthesis and many other fields. Continuously improving the performance of quantum computers will undoubtedly expand our understanding of the world and could open the door to a new era of technology.

Applications of quantum interference

Quantum interference is a phenomenon that arises from the basic principles of quantum mechanics. It illustrates how quantum particles, such as electrons, photons or entire atoms, can exhibit wave properties. This ability of particles to move through space and time, creating wave patterns that can overlap, leads to interference patterns that are normally associated with classical waves, such as water waves or sound waves.

Quantum parallelism

The unique ability of quantum computers to perform multiple calculations simultaneously is closely linked to the phenomenon of quantum interference. This property allows quantum computers to utilise their immense computing power and offers a fundamental advantage over classical computers.

Quantum interference makes it possible to superimpose the amplitudes of the wave functions corresponding to the different quantum states in such a way that constructive interference increases the probability of the desired results, while destructive interference reduces the probabilities of undesired results. Carefully designed quantum operations (quantum gates) can be used to adjust the phases of the qubits so that their wave functions interfere in the desired way at the end of the calculation. Examples of this are

- Shor's algorithm: Uses quantum interference to factorise large numbers efficiently. The interference patterns generated by the quantum calculations help to determine the periodicity of a function, which is a key step in factorisation.

- Grover's algorithm: A search algorithm that uses quantum interference to increase the probability of finding the correct search result in an unsorted database, resulting in a much faster solution than any classical algorithm.

The challenge in utilising quantum interference lies in the precise control of the qubit phases and maintaining the coherence of the qubits over time. Any form of decoherence can disrupt the interference patterns and impair computing performance. Advances in the areas of error correction, qubit design and system shielding are crucial to overcome these challenges and harness the full power of quantum interference.

Quantum cryptography

Quantum interference also plays an important role in quantum cryptography, especially in protocols such as BB84, which was designed for secure key exchange. While the BB84 protocol is mainly based on the principles of quantum uncertainty and no-cloning theory, the concept of quantum interference can play a central role in related quantum communication scenarios or in extensions of BB84 and other protocols based on interference effects.

At its core, the BB84 protocol utilises quantum uncertainty by sending and receiving quantum states in different bases. An eavesdropping attempt in this context inevitably disturbs the state of the qubits due to the measurement process, leading to recognisable errors in the key exchange. This perturbation can be interpreted as a change in expectations regarding quantum interference patterns, although the protocol is directly based on the impossibility of measuring the state of a quantum system without perturbation. More on this later.

In other contexts of quantum cryptography, such as quantum key distribution protocols explicitly based on quantum interference patterns, the role of quantum interference is more direct. Protocols based on the superposition and interference of quantum states utilise the sensitive interference patterns to monitor the integrity of the communication. Any interference by an eavesdropper alters the interference patterns in a way that can be detected by the communicating parties.

In protocols based on quantum interference, a series of qubits is typically sent in specially prepared states to generate specific interference patterns. An intervention or measurement attempt by a third party would disturb these patterns. This interference would manifest itself in an increased error rate in the transmitted data, signalling to the participants that the security of their communication has been compromised.

The further development of quantum cryptography could increasingly rely on the utilisation of quantum interference in order to develop even more secure communication protocols. As interference patterns are extremely sensitive to disturbances, they offer a powerful tool to ensure the security of transmitted information. Experiments and protocols based on distributed quantum interference could form the basis for future quantum communication networks that offer unprecedented security.

The use of quantum interference in practical applications also poses challenges, in particular the need to maintain high coherence rates of qubits over time. Any form of decoherence can disturb the interference patterns and thus affect the accuracy and reliability of quantum computations.

Conclusion

Quantum interference is a fundamental principle of quantum mechanics and forms the backbone of many technologies and methods in the world of quantum computing. By understanding and manipulating quantum interference patterns, researchers can push the boundaries of information processing and open up new possibilities in computer technology, cryptography and beyond. Despite the technical challenges associated with realising coherent and scalable quantum systems, further research into quantum interference promises exciting progress towards fully realising the potential of quantum computers.

Classical computers vs. quantum computers

The comparison between classical computers and quantum computers not only highlights the difference in the way they work, but also in their potential applications and limitations. While classical computers form the basis of today's digital technology, quantum computers offer a fundamentally new way of processing information based on the principles of quantum mechanics.

Basic working principles

The fundamental difference between classical computers and quantum computers lies in the way they process and store information. These differences open up potentials for quantum computers that go far beyond what is possible with classical computers, especially for certain types of problems.

Classical computers are based on bits as basic units of information. A bit is the smallest amount of data and can have one of two states: 0 or 1. These binary states are the basis of classical information processing, where complex calculations are performed by combining logical operations (such as AND, OR and NOT) on these bits. The performance of classic computers, from smartphones to supercomputers, is based on the increasing miniaturisation of bit-processing components, which leads to a steady increase in computing capacity. Nevertheless, classic computers remain fundamentally sequential in their computing capability, even if techniques such as parallel processing are used to increase efficiency.

Quantum computers, on the other hand, utilise quantum bits or qubits, which, unlike classical bits, apply the principles of quantum mechanics. A qubit can exist not only in the states 0 or 1, but also in a superposition of both states simultaneously. This superposition enables a single qubit to carry more information than a classical bit. In addition, qubits can be connected to each other through the phenomenon of quantum entanglement, whereby the state of one qubit can directly influence the state of another, regardless of the distance between them. These properties allow quantum computers to perform an enormous amount of calculations in parallel.

The use of quantum interference also enables quantum computers to select from a large number of possible calculation paths those that lead to the desired solution. This enables quantum computers to solve certain problems, such as the factorisation of large numbers (important for cryptography) or the simulation of quantum systems (important for materials science and pharmacy), potentially much faster than classical computers.

While classical computers remain indispensable to the general public and industry for tasks such as word processing, database management and many types of software development, quantum computers offer solutions to previously inaccessible problems. However, research and development in the field of quantum computing technology still faces significant technical challenges, including the stabilisation of qubits and the scaling of quantum systems.

Quantum computing is still at an early stage of development, but advances in quantum technology will revolutionise the way we think about data processing and problem-solving in the medium and long term. The parallel nature of quantum computation, together with the ability to perform complex simulations and enable new forms of cryptography, points to enormous potential beyond what is possible with classical computing technologies.

Calculation capacity and areas of application

The computational capacity and application areas of classical computers and quantum computers reflect the fundamentally different principles on which these technologies are based. Each has its own strengths and is better suited to certain types of tasks.

The strength of classic computers lies in their versatility and efficiency for a wide range of tasks. They are indispensable for everyday applications such as word processing, internet browsing, multimedia playback and running business software. They are also capable of performing complex scientific calculations and data analyses, which are of central importance in many areas of research and industry. Their architecture enables them to process large amounts of data quickly and efficiently, relying on a huge and ever-growing library of algorithms optimised for a variety of problems.

Quantum computers, on the other hand, are known for their potential advantages in specific, particularly computationally intensive problems. Their unique ability to utilise superposition states and entanglement enables them to find solutions to problems that classical computers would either not be able to solve at all or only with impractically high expenditure of time and energy:

- Factorisation of large numbers: Quantum computers could undermine the security of current cryptography systems based on the difficulty of this problem. Shor's algorithm, which runs on quantum computers, can factorise large numbers efficiently, which is practically impossible for classical computers.
- Searching in unsorted databases: Grover's algorithm demonstrates the ability of quantum computers to significantly improve the efficiency of searches in large, unsorted data sets by drastically reducing the number of steps required compared to classical algorithms.
- Simulation of quantum systems: Perhaps one of the most promising applications of quantum computers is the simulation of complex quantum systems. This could enable groundbreaking advances in materials science by allowing researchers to accurately predict the behaviour of atoms

and molecules in the development of new materials and medicines.

The potential applications of quantum computers could enable revolutionary advances in several fields:

- Materials science: The precise simulation of material properties at quantum level could lead to the development of new materials with customised properties.
- Cryptography: In addition to the risk of compromising existing encryption systems, quantum computers also provide the basis for new, theoretically unbreakable quantum encryption methods.
- Optimisation problems: Many areas of science and industry, from logistics to financial analysis, could benefit from quantum algorithms that solve optimisation problems more efficiently.

While classical computers remain the workhorses of information processing, quantum computers offer solutions to previously inaccessible challenges. The coexistence and integration of both technologies could redefine the boundaries of what is possible with computing and drive innovation in almost all areas of science and industry.

Scalability and stability

The differences in scalability and stability between classical computers and quantum computers emphasise the respective technological challenges and opportunities that characterise both areas.

Classic computers benefit from decades of development and optimisation when it comes to their architecture. Their scalability is based on relatively straightforward principles: More performance can often be achieved by adding more processors (or computing cores), more RAM or larger storage solutions. This modularity and expandability has led to the powerful and versatile computer systems that are now used in almost every aspect of modern life.

The stability and reliability of classic computers are also the result of extensive research and development. Advanced error correction mechanisms and robust data integrity techniques ensure that systems function correctly even in the event of hardware failures or external faults. These systems are designed to be fault-tolerant, which means that they can continue to operate even in the event of individual component failures.

Quantum computers, by contrast, face unique and significant challenges in terms of scalability and stability. The core principles that make quantum computers so powerful - superposition and entanglement - are also the source of their greatest challenges. Qubits must be kept in a precisely controlled quantum state, which is made extremely difficult by interactions with the environment (decoherence). This problem becomes more pronounced as the number of qubits and the complexity of quantum circuits increases.

Quantum error correction is a key element in overcoming the challenges of decoherence and other sources of error. In contrast to classical systems, where error correction is achieved through redundancy and simple correction algorithms, error correction in quantum systems requires more complex and subtle approaches. Since measuring a quantum state changes it, quantum error correction codes must be designed to detect and correct errors without disturbing the fragile quantum information.

Despite these challenges, the potential benefits of quantum computers are enormous, especially for tasks that overwhelm classical computers. Active research in areas such as quantum error correction, the development of more stable qubit designs and efficient algorithms for controlling quantum systems is gradually bringing the realisation of practical quantum computers closer. The parallel developments in classical computing technology and quantum computing technology promise a future in which both technologies are used in a complementary way to solve a wide range of problems, from basic research to practical applications in industry and technology.

Development status and accessibility

The development and use of classical computers compared to quantum computers clearly reflect the different levels of maturity and the different areas of application of these technologies.

The technology behind classic computers has evolved continuously over decades, resulting in an extraordinary variety of devices that are used in almost every aspect of daily life and in almost every industry. Classic computers are the foundation of the modern information society, enabling everything from basic communication and organisational tasks to complex scientific calculations and data analysis. Their technology is sophisticated and reliable, making them attractive to consumers and businesses alike. Thanks to the wide range of form factors available - from powerful servers that form the backbone of the Internet and large corporate networks to mobile devices that fit in your pocket - classic computers can be used flexibly in a variety of applications.

Quantum computers, on the other hand, offer revolutionary potential for solving certain categories of problems that classical computers either cannot solve or can only solve with prohibitively high effort. Despite significant advances in quantum computing technology and growing interest from both academia and industry, this technology is still at an early stage of development. Quantum computers are currently mainly research and development tools. Some models have been made available via cloud services, allowing researchers and developers around the world to experiment with quantum algorithms and explore the potential of this new form of computing. However, quantum computers are not yet ready for widespread use in practice. The challenges in terms of stability, scalability and susceptibility to errors require further intensive research and development.

While classical computers will continue to play a central role in our daily lives and in the global economy, scientists and engineers are working to push the boundaries of quantum computing technology. The vision is to develop quantum computers so that they can be used in a complementary way to classical computers, especially for tasks where they offer a unique advantage. This could herald a new era of information processing in which the combined strengths of both types of computers are used to solve complex problems in science, medicine, materials science and other fields that were previously inaccessible.

Classical computers and quantum computers are not direct competitors, but complement each other in many respects. Classical systems will remain indispensable for the vast majority of computing tasks and for everyday applications. Quantum computers, on the other hand, could offer solutions to problems that were previously considered insurmountable, opening up new horizons in science and technology. The future could see a combination of both approaches, with quantum and classical computers working together to maximise their respective strengths.

The development of quantum computers

Early phase of research and theoretical foundations

The early phase of research and the development of the theoretical foundations of quantum computing technology are closely linked to the fundamental discoveries in quantum mechanics. Quantum mechanics itself began to establish itself as a distinct field of physics in the early 20th century, with pioneering work by physicists such as Max Planck, Albert Einstein, Niels Bohr, Werner Heisenberg, Erwin Schrödinger and many others. These theoretical foundations formed the basis for understanding the unique and often non-intuitive behaviour of matter and energy at the smallest scales.

However, the idea of the quantum computer as we know it today only began to take shape in the 1980s. Some key moments and contributions have contributed significantly to the development of the theoretical foundations:

Richard Feynman (1981)

Richard Feynman, one of the most brilliant and influential physicists of the 20th century, played a decisive role in conceptualising the idea of quantum computing. His ideas and proposals laid the foundation for all subsequent developments in the field of quantum computing. During his famous speech at the Physics Conference in 1981, often cited as "Simulating Physics with

Computers", Feynman brought up a fundamental insight relating to the limitations of classical computers in simulating quantum mechanical systems.

Feynman argued that classical computers are inherently incapable of efficiently simulating quantum systems. The reason for this lies in the nature of quantum mechanics itself, which is characterised by superposition, entanglement and non-locality - phenomena that have no direct counterpart in the world of classical physics. A classical computer based on binary bits would have to use exponentially growing resources to even come close to capturing the state space of a quantum system.

Feynman's brilliant insight was that a computer that utilised quantum mechanical principles itself - i.e. a quantum computer - would be able to overcome these limitations. Such a device could natively simulate quantum systems by directly utilising the quantum mechanical properties of matter to perform calculations.

This idea was revolutionary because it paved the way for a completely new paradigm of information processing. Instead of trying to simulate quantum mechanics within the confines of a classical computational model, Feynman proposed using the rules of quantum mechanics itself as the basis for calculations and simulations. This opened up the theoretical possibility of tackling problems that are inaccessible to classical computers, including the simulation of molecules and materials, optimisation problems and the development of new types of quantum algorithms.

Feynman's lecture inspired generations of physicists, mathematicians and computer scientists to develop the concepts and technologies needed to realise quantum computers. Although the technical challenges are enormous and quantum computing technology is still in its infancy, ongoing research has already led to significant breakthroughs. It has also deepened our understanding of the fundamentals of quantum mechanics and its applications in information processing.

Feynman's visionary ideas are a shining example of how profound theoretical insights can shape the direction of scientific and technological development. His contribution to quantum computing remains a central legacy in the history of computer science and quantum physics.

David Deutsch (1985)

David Deutsch, a British physicist, played a crucial role in the development of the theoretical foundations of quantum computing with his formulation of the concept of the quantum Turing machine in the 1980s. This work, often regarded as a milestone in quantum computing technology, extended the classical Turing machine model, which forms the basis for understanding what it means to perform computation, into the quantum realm.

Deutsch's concept of the quantum Turing machine was the first rigorous attempt to extend the traditional model of the Turing machine - an abstract machine model that represents the principles of algorithmic computing - to quantum systems. While a classical Turing machine is based on binary states (bits) and uses deterministic transitions between these states, a quantum Turing machine uses quantum bits (qubits), which can be in superposition states, and processes information through quantum transitions.

Deutsch's work provided a formal basis for the theory of quantum computing and showed that quantum computers can potentially solve certain types of problems more efficiently than classical computers. A key difference between classical and quantum Turing machines lies in their ability to perform calculations in parallel. Due to the quantum phenomena of superposition and entanglement, quantum Turing machines can perform an exponential number of computations simultaneously, which gives them a theoretical advantage for certain problems.

Deutsch's ideas opened the door for the development of specific quantum algorithms that utilise the unique properties of quantum computers. Examples include Shor's algorithm for factoring large numbers and Grover's algorithm for searching unsorted databases. Both algorithms demonstrate the superiority of quantum computers over classical computers for specific problems.

By formulating the concept of the quantum Turing machine, David Deutsch not only laid the theoretical foundation for quantum computing, but also provided the conceptual framework that made it possible to explore the limits and possibilities of this new form of information processing. His work has shown that the principles of quantum mechanics not only reveal fascinating physical phenomena, but can also have practical applications in information processing that have the potential to fundamentally change the landscape of computer technology.

Peter Shor (1994)

Peter Shor, an American mathematician and professor at the Massachusetts Institute of Technology (MIT), made a groundbreaking breakthrough in quantum computer technology with the development of the Shor algorithm named after him in 1994. This algorithm demonstrates the ability of a quantum computer to factorise large numbers into their prime factors in a time that scales polynomially with the length of the numbers. This is in stark contrast to the best known algorithms for classical computers, whose running time increases exponentially with the length of the number to be factorised.

Factorisation of large numbers is a classical problem in number theory, but it has practical applications in cryptography, especially in the context of the widely used RSA encryption method. RSA security is based on the assumption that the factorisation of a large number, which is the product of two large prime numbers, is practically impossible for classical computers. Shor's discovery showed that this assumption is no longer tenable in the age of quantum computers, as an efficient quantum algorithm exists that can solve this task.

The potential ability of quantum computers to execute the Shor algorithm has profound implications for the security of most of today's cryptographic systems. It emphasises the need to develop new cryptographic schemes that remain secure in the era of quantum computers, known as post-quantum cryptography.

The development of the Shor algorithm acted as a catalyst for interest and investment in quantum computing technology. The prospect of solving practical problems inaccessible to classical computers motivated both academic research and industry to drive the development of quantum computers. This led to a significant increase in efforts to realise practical quantum computers, including the development of hardware, error correction mechanisms and other algorithms that exploit the unique advantages of quantum computers.

Peter Shor's work on the Shor algorithm marks a turning point in the history of quantum computing and emphasises the transformative potential of this technology. While practical quantum computers capable of executing the Shor algorithm for large numbers do not yet exist, the mere possibility of such computations has already had a profound impact on the direction of cryptographic research and data security strategies. Shor's contribution remains a shining example of the connection between theoretical computer science and physics and its impact on technology and society.

Lov Grover (1996)

Lov Grover, a researcher at Bell Labs, made a significant contribution to the development of quantum computing technology by presenting an algorithm in 1996 that is now known as Grover's algorithm. This algorithm shows how quantum computers can search an unsorted database much more efficiently than classical computers. While a classical computer has to search through half of all the entries in the database on average to find the desired element, Grover's algorithm only needs around the square root of the number of entries to achieve the same result.

Grover's algorithm uses quantum mechanics, in particular the phenomenon of quantum superposition, to perform a parallel search through all entries in the database simultaneously. Through a clever sequence of quantum operations known as amplitude amplification, the algorithm systematically increases the probability of finding the element being searched for, while decreasing the probabilities for all other elements. After a series of iterations of the algorithm, the element being searched for is identified with high probability when the measurement of the quantum system is performed.

Grover's algorithm is an excellent example of the type of problem where quantum computers offer a distinct advantage over classical computers. It is important to emphasise that the algorithm offers a quadratic speed advantage, meaning that it can significantly speed up searches in large databases. This is in contrast to the exponential speed advantages observed with other quantum algorithms, such as the Shor algorithm. Nevertheless, the speed advantage is significant in practice and demonstrates the potential of quantum computers to solve certain classes of problems more efficiently.

Although Grover's algorithm was developed specifically for the task of database search, its fundamental technique - amplitude amplification - has found wider applications in other areas, including machine learning, optimisation problems and the development of new quantum algorithms. The general principles behind Grover's work have shown how quantum parallelism and interference can be used to achieve algorithmic improvements beyond classical approaches.

Grover's algorithm remains a key element in the theory of quantum computing and a shining example of the practical possibilities of this emerging technology. It illustrates not only how quantum mechanics can be used to solve everyday problems, but also how quantum computers are capable of pushing the boundaries of classical information processing. While the full realisation of this technology is still in the future, Grover's contribution provides a solid foundation for understanding and further exploring the potential of quantum computing.

Although the theoretical foundations for quantum computing are now firmly established, research faces considerable challenges when it comes to practical implementation. These include the generation and maintenance of qubits in coherent states, the scaling of quantum systems, error correction in a quantum context and the development of efficient quantum algorithms.

In parallel, theoretical developments in areas such as quantum error correction and the development of new quantum algorithms have helped to address the practical hurdles and pave the way for the realisation of functional quantum computers.

The early phase of research and theoretical foundations of quantum computing technology reflect a profound shift in our understanding of computation and information processing. While the first concepts and algorithms demonstrated the immense potential power of quantum computing, scientists around the world continue to overcome technical and theoretical challenges to bring this technology to full maturity. The journey from the fundamental principles of quantum mechanics to practical quantum computers is a fascinating example of the transformation of abstract scientific concepts into revolutionary technologies.

The development of the first quantum algorithms

The development of the first quantum algorithms marked a turning point in the history of computer science and physics by translating the theoretical potential of quantum computers into practical computational advantages. These algorithms illustrate how the basic principles of quantum mechanics - superposition, entanglement and interference - can be used to solve problems in ways that are beyond the reach of classical computers. Here is an overview of the pioneering first quantum algorithms and their significance:

Deutsch's algorithm (1985)

David Deutsch developed the first quantum algorithm, known as Deutsch's algorithm, which solves a specific problem: to determine whether a given binary function is constant or balanced. Although this problem is not of practical importance in itself, the algorithm demonstrated for the first time the possibility of using quantum parallelism for information processing by solving the problem with a single operation - a process that would have required two operations by classical means.

German-Jozsa algorithm (1992)

Expanded by Richard Jozsa, the Deutsch-Jozsa algorithm extended the original problem to functions with
multiple inputs and thus became the first example of a
quantum algorithm that shows an exponential advantage over any possible deterministic classical algorithm. It impressively demonstrates the superiority of
quantum computers for certain types of computational
problems, even if these problems are mainly of academic
interest.

Shor's Algorithm (1994)

Peter Shor's development of a quantum algorithm for
factoring large numbers and finding discrete logarithms
provided the first strong evidence of the practical benefits of quantum computing. Shor's algorithm can factorise large numbers exponentially faster than the best
known classical algorithms, which has important implications for cryptography, especially for encryption systems such as RSA, which are based on the difficulty of
factoring large numbers.

Grover's Algorithm (1996)

Lov Grover's algorithm for accelerating searches in an
unsorted database offered a quadratic speed advantage
over classical search algorithms. This algorithm showed
that quantum computers can offer advantages not only

for specialised mathematical problems, but also for more general computational problems.

Significance of the early quantum algorithms

These first quantum algorithms played a crucial role in formulating the theory and potential of quantum computing. They provided proof that quantum computers are capable of outperforming classical computers in certain computational tasks and motivated both theoretical and practical research in this emerging field. Although many of these early algorithms solved academic problems, they laid the foundation for the development of further quantum algorithms with direct practical applications and were instrumental in increasing interest and investment in quantum computing technology.

Quantum superiority (2016)

Google announces that its quantum processor Sycamore has solved a specific computational task that is virtually unsolvable for classical supercomputers, a milestone often referred to as "quantum supremacy". More on this later.

Development of quantum hardware

The development of quantum hardware is a rapidly evolving process that encompasses a variety of approaches and technologies. Progress in this area is crucial for the realisation of practical quantum computers.

Superconducting qubits

Companies such as IBM, Google and Rigetti are leading the way in the development of quantum computers based on superconducting circuits. This technology has established itself as one of the most promising approaches for the realisation of practically usable quantum computers. The choice of superconducting circuits for the generation of qubits brings several advantages, particularly in terms of scalability and advances in error correction.

Superconducting qubits utilise the unique properties of superconducting materials that can conduct electrical current without resistance. By applying microwave radiation to these circuits, states can be generated that are suitable for performing quantum computations. These qubits can be produced relatively easily using lithographic processes similar to those used in the semiconductor industry, which facilitates their integration into larger systems.

One of the main advantages of superconducting qubits is their relative ease of scaling. Since the technology shares compatible manufacturing methods with the existing semiconductor industry, it is theoretically easier to develop systems with a larger number of qubits. IBM, Google and Rigetti have already presented demonstrations of quantum processors with dozens of qubits, underlining the feasibility of this approach.

Another crucial area in which significant progress has been made is error correction. While superconducting qubits are sensitive to external perturbations that can lead to errors, the use of quantum error correction codes allows these errors to be detected and corrected. Companies such as Google have made significant progress in the development and implementation of such error correction methods, which are essential for the realisation of reliable quantum computations.

Despite progress, there are still challenges, particularly in terms of susceptibility to errors and the need for extremely cold operating temperatures to maintain superconductivity. These requirements increase the complexity and cost of quantum computing systems.

Trapped Ions

The development of quantum computers based on trapped ion technology is a promising area of research.

Start-ups such as IonQ and numerous academic research groups worldwide are dedicated to this approach, which is characterised by long coherence times and high fidelity of quantum operations. These properties make ion trap quantum computers particularly attractive for a variety of applications that require precise and reliable quantum information processing.

Trapped ions provide an excellent basis for the realisation of quantum computers thanks to their stable quantum states and the ability to maintain them over long periods of time. The high fidelity of the quantum operations performed between the ions supports the execution of complex calculations with minimal error, which is crucial for the reliability of the results. In addition, the technology enables unique flexibility and reconfigurability of the qubit arrays, which is achieved by precisely controlling the electromagnetic traps in which the ions are held.

Despite these promising properties, developers of ion trap quantum computers face significant technical challenges. The complex nature of trapping and manipulating individual ions requires sophisticated techniques and equipment, which complicates the development and maintenance of such systems. In addition, the scaling of this technology, although theoretically feasible, is fraught with difficulties in practice. Ensuring the effective integration and interaction of a large number of qubits in a single coherent system remains one of the main challenges for researchers in this field.

However, ongoing efforts to solve these challenges point to the great potential of ion trap quantum computers.

The work of companies such as IonQ and research groups worldwide shows significant progress towards practical quantum computers. In the near future, these could herald a revolution in fields such as materials science, optimisation and cryptography by providing solutions to problems that are inaccessible to classical computers. Development in this area therefore remains an exciting field with the prospect of ground-breaking technological breakthroughs.

Quantum dots

Quantum dots, which are used in quantum computer technology, represent an innovative and promising approach for the realisation of quantum computers. Due to their unique physical properties, these nanoscopically small semiconductor particles offer the possibility of representing quantum bits or qubits. The size and shape of a quantum dot determine its electronic properties, including the energy levels of its electrons, which makes them particularly attractive for use in quantum information processing.

A key advantage of quantum dots is their potential compatibility with existing semiconductor manufacturing processes. Since they can be manufactured from materials already used in the semiconductor industry, this opens up the possibility of producing quantum computers using established micro- and nanofabrication techniques. This compatibility promises not only good scalability, as many qubits can be integrated on a single chip, but also a reduction in production costs, which could be decisive for the commercial development of quantum computer technologies.

Despite these promising prospects, researchers and engineers working on the development of quantum computers based on quantum dots face considerable challenges. One of the biggest challenges is the precise control of quantum dot properties. The production of quantum dots with precisely defined sizes, shapes and compositions is crucial to achieve the desired quantum states and properties. Any irregularities can lead to unpredictable behaviour of the qubits and increase the system's susceptibility to errors.

Another critical problem is maintaining the coherence of the qubits. In an environment that is inherently susceptible to interference, quantum dots must be protected from external influences such as thermal fluctuations and electromagnetic radiation that could disrupt sensitive quantum states and shorten coherence times. The development of techniques to isolate and protect quantum dots from such interference is therefore crucial for the realisation of practical quantum computers.

Research into quantum dots for quantum computing technology is still at a relatively early stage, but progress in this area could lay the foundations for a new generation of quantum computers that are both powerful and scalable. Continued efforts in materials science, nanotechnology and quantum physics are crucial to overcoming the challenges and realising the full potential of quantum dots.

Photons

The use of photons to represent qubits in quantum information processing, especially in quantum communication and cryptography, offers unique advantages.

Photons, the basic building blocks of light, are ideally suited for the transmission of quantum information over long distances. One of the main advantages is their ability to be transported at room temperature and over long distances without suffering significant decoherence. This property makes photons ideal candidates for the realisation of secure quantum communication networks and for the development of technologies such as the quantum internet.

Another key advantage of photonic qubits is their immunity to many types of environmental interference that typically affect electronic systems. Photons are not susceptible to electromagnetic interference in the way that electronic qubits can be, making them particularly useful for applications in quantum cryptography. For example, protocols such as the BB84 protocol for quantum key exchange utilise the unique quantum properties of photons to enable theoretically secure communication. Any attempts at eavesdropping would inevitably disrupt the quantum states of the photons, making them detectable.

Despite these promising properties, the development of photonic quantum computers and communication systems faces a major challenge: realising the effective interaction of photons with each other. In contrast to matter-based qubits, which can interact with each other relatively easily, photons tend to pass each other without interaction. However, to perform quantum computations, it is necessary for qubits to interact with each other in a controlled manner to implement quantum gates. Achieving strong interactions between photons requires the use of special techniques and materials, such as nonlinear optical media or the use of quantum dots and other nanomaterials as mediators.

Research in this area is focussed on developing innovative methods to overcome this challenge. Approaches such as the use of entangled photon pairs, the development of photonic crystals to control the propagation of light and the use of cavity quantum electrodynamics (QED) systems are just some of the strategies being explored to enable effective photon-photon interactions. Advances in photonics and quantum optics are crucial for the realisation of these technologies and could pave the way for the development of highly secure quantum communication networks and powerful quantum computers based on the use of photons.

NV centres in diamonds

Nitrogen vacancies (NV centres) in diamonds represent a direction in quantum computing technology that has the potential to realise robust and practical quantum systems. NV centres are formed when two neighbouring carbon atoms in the diamond structure are replaced by a nitrogen atom and a vacancy (a missing carbon atom). These defects have unique electronic properties that make them particularly suitable for quantum information processing.

One of the most notable advantages of NV centres is their ability to operate at room temperature. Unlike many other qubit systems that require extremely low temperatures for stable operation, NV centres can function in a much wider temperature range. This greatly simplifies the technical requirements for quantum computing systems and makes them potentially more accessible and practical for a wide range of applications.

In addition, NV centres offer relatively long coherence times. The coherence time of a qubit is a measure of how long it can maintain its quantum state before it is perturbed by environmental influences. Longer coherence times are crucial for performing complex quantum computations, as they give researchers more time to perform quantum operations before decoherence occurs.

Despite these advantages, researchers face considerable challenges when working with NV centres. One of the greatest difficulties lies in the precise manipulation and control of NV centres. Precise control of the quantum states of these defects requires sophisticated optical and magnetic techniques that still need to be further developed and refined to enable reliable and efficient quantum information processing.

Another significant challenge is the integration of NV centres on a larger scale. While individual NV centres can act as qubits, a practical quantum computer requires precise control over a large network of qubits that can interact with each other. The development of techniques to scale and network NV centres without compromising their coherence properties is an active area of research.

Research and development in the field of NV centres in diamonds is promising and could lead to quantum computers that are robust, functional at room temperature and relatively easy to handle. Advances in materials science, nanotechnology and quantum physics play a crucial role in overcoming the existing challenges. Solving these problems could pave the way for new quantum computing platforms that can be used for a wide range of applications, from quantum simulation to quantum cryptography and sensor technology.

Topological qubits

Topological qubits represent a particularly exciting and advanced approach in quantum computing technology. Their development is based on the concept of topological quantum matter and utilises the mathematical theory of topology to create a new form of qubit that is inherently protected against many types of perturbations and errors. This property makes topological qubits particularly promising for creating robust, scalable quantum computers that are less susceptible to decoherence and errors that affect the reliability and efficiency of conventional quantum systems.

At the heart of topological qubits lies the use of quasiparticles known as anions, which can occur in certain two-dimensional materials under specific conditions. Anions have the remarkable property that their exchange (i.e. the movement of one anion around another) changes the state of the system in a way that depends only on the topological class of the exchange path, not on the precise details of the path. These exchange operations, known as "braiding", change the state of the system in a predictable and robust way, which can be used to realise quantum computations.

The biggest advantage of topological qubits lies in their theoretical fault tolerance. Since the information is stored in the global topological properties of the system, local perturbations that typically lead to errors in quantum computers are less likely to affect these states. This significantly reduces the need for complex error correction codes that are required in other quantum computing systems.

However, the realisation of topological qubits faces considerable scientific and technical challenges. The existence of the anions required for topological qubits must be proven in practical systems and made controllable. Currently, materials that could harbour so-called Majorana fermions - a class of anions that are particularly suitable for the generation of topological qubits - are the subject of intensive research. In addition, the manipulation and readout of states encoded in the topological properties of materials requires innovative techniques and approaches.

Despite these challenges, the topological approach offers a perspective for the future of quantum computing technology, with the potential to create quantum computers that are more powerful and reliable than ever before. The successful development of topological qubits could lead to a revolution in quantum information processing, with far-reaching applications in cryptography, materials science, and beyond. Research in this area is cutting-edge and combines concepts from quantum physics, materials science, mathematics and computer science, opening up the possibility of redefining the limits of what is possible with computers.

Selection of technology

The choice of technology for the development of qubits and thus quantum computers is a decision rooted in the requirements of the intended quantum computing tasks as well as in the physical and technical capabilities of the different qubit systems. Each qubit technology brings its own specific advantages, challenges and potential areas of application, ranging from basic properties such as coherence times, operation speed and scalability to compatibility with the existing technological infrastructure.

Superconducting qubits and trapped ions are two of the most advanced technologies in quantum computing. Superconducting qubits benefit from relatively easy integration into existing semiconductor manufacturing processes and are already showing impressive results in prototype quantum computers developed by leading technology companies and research organisations. Their coherence times and operation speeds are promising for many applications, although scaling beyond hundreds or thousands of qubits still poses challenges.

Trapped ions, with their long coherence times and high operational accuracies, represent another promising approach. They have proven to be extremely precise in performing quantum operations and offer the possibility of developing stable quantum computers. The main challenges here are scaling and integration into a practical quantum computer system that works efficiently and reliably.

Quantum dots and photonic qubits are at an earlier stage of development compared to superconducting qubits and trapped ions. Quantum dots offer an exciting prospect due to their potential compatibility with existing semiconductor processes and their potential room temperature operation. The challenges here lie in the precise control of quantum states and integration into larger systems. Photonic qubits, which are particularly promising for quantum communication and cryptography, face the challenge of finding effective methods for the interaction between photons, which is necessary for performing complex quantum computations.

Quantum communication and cryptography

Quantum communication and quantum cryptography represent applications of quantum mechanics that have the potential to fundamentally change the way information is securely transmitted. Quantum key distribution in particular is an area where significant progress has already been made, leading to the development of the first commercial systems. These systems utilise fundamental principles of quantum mechanics to enable theoretically secure communication.

Quantum encryption

The development of the first commercial quantum key distribution systems (QKD) marks an important milestone on the way to theoretically secure communication.

QKD systems utilise the unique principles of quantum mechanics, in particular quantum entanglement and indeterminacy, to enable the secure transmission of encryption keys between two parties. At the core of this technology lies the property that any observation or measurement of a quantum system inevitably changes its state. This means that any attempt to intercept the quantum information used for the key exchange is recognised by the communication partners.

Unlike traditional cryptographic methods, whose security is based on the computational difficulty of solving certain mathematical problems (such as the factorisation of large numbers), the security of QKD is based on the fundamental laws of quantum physics. This provides a form of security that is considered future-proof, as it cannot be compromised by technological advances.

The first commercial QKD systems offer promising applications for a variety of industries that require secure communication channels. These include the financial sector, government security organisations and operators of critical infrastructures. By ensuring secure key distribution, QKD systems can help protect the confidentiality and integrity of sensitive information.

Despite the impressive potential of QKD, the technology and its implementation face challenges. These include the need to increase the range and efficiency of the systems and to reduce the cost of implementation. However, advances in quantum communication technology, including the development of satellite-based QKD systems and the integration of QKD into existing optical networks, suggest that these challenges can increasingly be overcome.

Ongoing research and development in the field of quantum communication promises to further improve the capabilities and availability of QKD systems. With the ongoing miniaturisation of the technology and integration into existing communication infrastructures, QKD systems could play an increasingly important role in ensuring global communication security. The future of quantum communication and cryptography therefore looks promising, with the potential to usher in a new era of communication security based on the immutable principles of quantum mechanics.

Quantum Internet

The development of a quantum internet represents one of the most fascinating and at the same time most challenging advances in modern communications technology.

This ambitious goal is based on the principles of quantum mechanics, in particular the phenomenon of quantum entanglement already described, which provides the basis for a revolutionary way of transmitting information.

A quantum internet uses quantum entanglement to transmit information between two points via so-called quantum bits or qubits without the information having to physically travel between the two points. This not only expands the bandwidth of information transmission, but also increases security, as any form of eavesdropping would disrupt the quantum states and thus make them immediately recognisable.

However, the realisation of such a quantum network requires ground-breaking advances in quantum technology. Research initiatives around the world, including government projects, academic institutions and private companies, are investing significant resources in overcoming technical challenges. These include the development of quantum repeaters needed to bridge long distances, the reliable generation and manipulation of entangled states and integration with existing tele-communications infrastructures.

A key application of a quantum internet is the creation of communication networks that are theoretically secure against any form of cyber-attack. Using quantum en-cryption, a direct application of quantum entanglement, messages could be transmitted in such a way that they can only be read by the intended recipient in their original state. Any attempt to intercept the transmitted information would change the quantum states and thus reveal the presence of the eavesdropper.

Although the vision of a fully realised quantum internet is still a long way off, the ongoing research and development projects mark significant steps towards this goal. The successful implementation of such a system could fundamentally change the way we think about data transmission and security, ushering in a new era of communication based on the fundamental principles of quantum mechanics. Progress in this area is being watched with great excitement as it has the potential to revolutionise the landscape of global communications and security.

The quantum internet promises to take communication technology far beyond the limits of conventional data transmission. It is based on the principles of quantum mechanics, in particular quantum entanglement, which makes it possible to share information between partners over any distance without this information having to use a conventional transmission path. This revolutionary concept offers numerous applications and benefits that could significantly improve both the security and efficiency of data transmission.

Areas of application

- Quantum cryptography and secure communication: Probably the most immediate and obvious application of a quantum internet is quantum cryptography, in particular the Quantum Key Distribution (QKD) protocol. QKD allows two parties to share a secure communication key that is immune to eavesdropping attempts. The security is based on the laws of quantum mechanics, which state that measuring a quantum state changes that state. An intruder can therefore not go unnoticed.
- Secure cloud computing: In a world where cloud services are becoming increasingly important, a quantum internet could significantly improve the security of these services. Data could be stored and transmitted in quantum states, protecting it from hacking and unauthorised access.
- Distributed quantum computing networks: Quantum computers promise to solve problems that are practically unsolvable for classical computers. A quantum internet could connect quantum computers over long distances, improving

their computing capacity and efficiency through distributed computing.

- Improved sensors and telescopes: Quantum entanglement can also be used to increase the sensitivity of sensors and telescopes. A quantum internet could facilitate the coordination of such devices over long distances, which could lead to a better understanding of the universe in astronomy, for example.

Advantages

- Unbreakable security: The main advantage of a quantum internet lies in its security. The transmission of information about quantum states and entanglements is in principle secure against any unauthorised access, as any measurement or disturbance of the state would be immediately detectable.
- High efficiency: Quantum communication could be more efficient than traditional communication methods as it is able to transmit and process multiple states simultaneously. This could lead to a significant increase in transmission capacities.
- Global range: Another significant advantage is the ability to transmit information over any distance almost instantaneously. This is in contrast to conventional communication methods, where the transmission speed is limited by the distance and the transmission media.

- Advancing scientific research: A quantum internet would also advance scientific research by opening up new possibilities for experiments in quantum physics and related disciplines. It could help answer some of the fundamental questions of physics and lead to the development of new technologies.

Overall, the quantum internet is a breakthrough technology that has the potential to fundamentally change the way we think about communication, security and data processing. While practical implementation still poses some challenges, researchers around the world are already working to realise the vision of a global, secure and efficient quantum internet.

Scalable quantum systems

The development of scalable quantum systems is one of the central areas of research in quantum computing. These systems should be able to effectively manipulate and control a large number of qubits in order to perform complex calculations that go far beyond the capabilities of classical computers.

Two crucial aspects on this path are advances in error correction and in the system architecture of quantum computers. These developments are essential in order to realise large-scale, fault-tolerant quantum computers.

Progress in error correction

Quantum computers are susceptible to errors caused by decoherence and quantum noise, which is due to the interaction of the qubits with their environment. Since the information is stored in quantum states, even the slightest external influences can disturb these states and distort the stored information. Advances in error correction are therefore crucial in order to be able to carry out reliable calculations with quantum computers.

Quantum error correction codes are complex and usually require the use of multiple physical qubits to make a single logical qubit fault tolerant. These codes allow the system to detect and correct errors without measuring or disturbing the quantum information itself. The development of efficient error correction mechanisms is one of the biggest challenges on the way to scalable quantum systems, as it involves a significant number of additional qubits and increased system complexity.

Improvements in the system architecture

The architecture of a quantum computer plays a decisive role in its scalability and performance. In contrast to classical computers, whose architecture is relatively standardised, there are a variety of approaches to quantum computers, including systems based on superconducting qubits, ion traps, topological qubits and photons.

Each of these technologies has its own advantages and disadvantages in terms of susceptibility to errors, coherence times, scalability and controllability. The selection and optimisation of the system architecture depends on the application for which the quantum computer is being developed. Advances in materials science, nanotechnology and optical technology are contributing to the development of architectures that can reliably control and link a larger number of qubits.

The integration of error-correcting codes into the system architecture is another important step. This requires close collaboration between the fields of quantum hardware and algorithmic development to ensure that the systems are not only large and powerful, but also practical to use.

Outlook

The realisation of large-scale, fault-tolerant quantum computers would represent a quantum leap in information processing. Such systems could solve tasks in the fields of materials science, drug development, optimisation problems and cryptography in a way that is unattainable for classical systems. Despite the enormous technical challenges that still need to be overcome, continuous progress in error correction and system architecture makes the future realisation of such quantum computers increasingly likely. Research and development in these areas is crucial to push the boundaries of what is possible with computer technology and to fully realise the enormous potential of quantum computing.

Quantum algorithms for practical applications

The research and development of quantum algorithms that offer specific advantages over classical algorithms is a promising field within quantum computing. These algorithms are designed to exploit the unique properties of quantum computers to solve problems in various fields such as materials science, optimisation problems and machine learning more efficiently.

Materials science

In materials science, quantum algorithms could be used to simulate and analyse the properties of complex molecules and materials at a quantum level. These simulations are extremely computationally intensive or even impossible for classical computers, as the number of possible states in a quantum system grows exponentially with the number of particles. However, quantum computers can utilise the superposition of states to simulate such systems directly and efficiently. This could pave the way for the discovery of new materials, the development of high-performance batteries, improved solar cells and novel drugs.

Optimisation problems

Optimisation problems are ubiquitous in many areas of industry and science, from logistics and engineering to finance. Quantum computers offer the possibility of finding solutions to such problems faster by exploring a wide range of potential solutions simultaneously and quickly identifying the optimal or near-optimal solutions through quantum interference. For example, quantum algorithms could help to increase the efficiency of supply chains, reduce manufacturing costs or solve complex network problems.

Machine learning

In the field of machine learning, quantum algorithms could help to improve the speed and efficiency of learning algorithms. Quantum computers could be used, for example, in pattern recognition, the optimisation of machine learning models or the acceleration of data-intensive processes such as the training of deep neural networks. With the ability to process large amounts of data simultaneously and perform complex calculations, quantum computers could revolutionise the way we use machine learning and artificial intelligence.

However, the development of these algorithms faces considerable challenges. These include the need to adapt the algorithms to the still limited capabilities and resources of current quantum computers, as well as the development of new theoretical frameworks and techniques for quantum programming. Despite these challenges, the potential of quantum algorithms is enormous and research in this area is being intensively pursued worldwide. Progress in this field could not only lead to significant scientific and technological breakthroughs, but also enable entirely new business models and industries.

Overall, we may be on the cusp of a new era of computing technology in which quantum computers and their customised algorithms will enable real-world problems to be solved in ways that were previously unimaginable. Research in the coming years will be crucial to unlock the full potential of this technology and develop practical applications for society.

Demonstration of quantum superiority

The demonstration of quantum supremacy is a significant milestone in the development of quantum computing technology. Quantum superiority refers to the point at which a quantum computer can solve a specific task faster or more efficiently than the most powerful classical supercomputer available. This concept is not only an important indicator of practical progress in quantum computing technology, but also proof of the theoretical potential of quantum computers to solve problems that are inaccessible to classical computers.

Google's Sycamore processor

In 2019, Google announced a breakthrough in quantum computing technology with its 54-qubit Sycamore processor.

Google claimed to have achieved quantum supremacy by performing a specific computational task in about 200 seconds that would take the world's most powerful traditional supercomputer, the IBM Summit, about 10,000 years. Although the task solved by the Sycamore processor was only of academic interest and had no practical application, it clearly demonstrated the ability of quantum computers to perform calculations that are beyond the reach of classical computers.

Google's announcement marked a historic moment for the quantum computing community and the wider scientific world, but also sparked a debate about the definition and meaning of quantum supremacy. Some experts and companies, including IBM, pointed out that the specific task Google had chosen for their proof had no direct practical use and that the methods for estimating the time classical computers would take to complete the task were unclear.

Regardless of the debates, Google's demonstration of quantum superiority has a symbolic meaning: it shows that quantum computers have the potential to go far beyond the limits of classical information processing. This success has increased interest and investment in quantum computing technology worldwide, leading to accelerated research and development activities in both academia and industry.

Achieving quantum supremacy is only a first step on the long road to developing fully functional and practical quantum computers. The challenges ahead include scaling quantum systems, improving fault tolerance and developing algorithms that can solve real-world problems. Despite these challenges, the demonstration of quantum superiority has strengthened the field and reaffirmed that quantum computing is a viable and promising future technology.

Advances in quantum computing technology and the increasing demonstration of practical applications indicate that quantum computers could play an increasingly important role in various fields in the coming years, from materials science and pharmacy to the optimisation of complex systems.

Areas of application for quantum computers

Materials Science

Materials science is one of the most promising application areas for quantum computing. This field, which is concerned with the discovery and development of new materials, could benefit significantly from the unique capabilities of quantum computing technology. The complexity of matter at the atomic and molecular level involves calculations that are either extremely time-consuming or simply impossible for classical computers. This is where quantum computers offer a decisive advantage.

One of the fundamental problems in materials science is the simulation of quantum systems. Classical computers reach their limits when it comes to the exact modelling of systems containing more than a few dozen quantum particles (electrons and atomic nuclei). Quantum computers, on the other hand, can overcome these limitations as they are able to simulate the quantum mechanical states directly. By using quantum superposition and entanglement, quantum computers can model complex molecules and materials in a way that reflects nature much more accurately.

The ability to precisely simulate materials at quantum level has the potential to revolutionise the development of new materials. Scientists could predict the properties of materials without having to perform time-consuming and costly physical experiments. This could accelerate the discovery of new, high-performance materials for electronics, energy generation and storage, as well as for pharmaceutical products. For example, the search for materials with high conductivity for superconductors or more efficient solar cells could be significantly simplified.

Development of new drugs

The application of quantum computers in pharmacy and drug development is exemplary of the transformative potential that this technology has in biomedical research and beyond.

The ability of quantum computers to simulate the interactions between molecules at a fundamental, quantum mechanical level opens up completely new horizons in drug discovery and development. This approach could fundamentally change traditional methods, which are often time-consuming, cost-intensive and subject to a high error rate.

The development of new drugs today is a lengthy and costly process that can often take more than a decade from discovery to market launch and can cost billions. A significant part of this time and resources is spent on identifying and optimising compounds that can effectively influence specific target structures in the human body. Quantum computers could speed up this process by making it possible to rapidly screen an enormous number of potential drug molecules and precisely calculate their interactions with biological targets. This would not only reduce the time and cost of drug discovery, but also increase the success rate in the early phases of drug development.

Another significant advantage of quantum computing technology is the ability to understand the dynamics of molecules and the complexity of biological systems in more detail. By simulating the quantum mechanical properties of molecules, scientists can better predict how a drug will work in the body, including its effectiveness and potential side effects. This could facilitate the development of safer and more effective drugs by helping to screen out candidates with undesirable properties at an early stage.

The high cost of drug development is partly due to the low success rates in the clinical phases. By more accurately predicting the efficacy and safety of drug candidates, quantum computing could help to improve these success rates and thus reduce the average cost and risk of developing new drugs. In the long term, this could lead to a more diversified pipeline of drugs and facilitate access to new therapies for patients worldwide.

The potential of quantum computers in pharmacy and drug development is enormous, but their full realisation is still to come. Current quantum computers are still at an early stage of development and further advances in quantum technology, algorithms and molecular biology are needed to realise this potential. Nevertheless, pharmaceutical companies and research institutes are showing great interest in quantum computing technology, and the first successes in simulating simple molecules point the way to a revolutionary change in the discovery and development of new drugs. The coming years could bring decisive breakthroughs that will sustainably improve the efficiency, safety and cost-effectiveness of drug research.

Personalised medicine

Personalised medicine, tailored to a patient's individual genetic, environmental and lifestyle factors, is at the heart of a revolutionary change in healthcare.

Quantum computers could play a key role in this area by expanding and accelerating the capabilities of personalised medicine. The unique power of quantum computers to simulate complex systems and analyse huge data sets makes them a valuable tool for the development and implementation of personalised medical treatments and therapies.

Genetic analysis is a central aspect of personalised medicine. Quantum computers could revolutionise the analysis of the human genome by significantly reducing the time it takes to sequence and interpret genetic data. This would make it possible to identify genetic predispositions to certain diseases more quickly and to develop customised treatment plans that are tailored to an individual's genetic constitution.

Quantum computers offer the potential to transform drug discovery and development by enabling accurate predictions of the interactions between drugs and patients' individual biological systems. This could lead to more efficient identification of drug candidates suitable for the treatment of specific genetic mutations. Such customised therapies could be more effective and associated with fewer side effects than conventional treatments.

Treatment in personalised medicine is based not only on genetic information, but also on a variety of data, including environmental factors, lifestyle and previous medical history. Quantum computers could help analyse these complex data sets to create detailed and individually tailored treatment plans. With the ability to recognise patterns in large and complex data sets, quantum computers could help improve the effectiveness of treatments while reducing costs.

Another significant contribution of quantum computers to personalised medicine could lie in the simulation of complex biological systems. By accurately simulating interactions at the molecular level, quantum computers could provide researchers with a better understanding of how diseases develop and progress on an individual basis. This knowledge could lead to the development of more precise diagnostic tools and more effective, personalised therapies.

Chemistry

Chemistry is another promising area of application for quantum computers that has the potential to bring about fundamental changes in research, development and production.

Quantum chemistry, which deals with the application of quantum mechanics to chemical problems, offers a rich field for the application of quantum computing technology. Quantum computers may be able to solve problems that are inaccessible to classical computers, expanding our understanding of chemical processes at the molecular level and accelerating the development of new materials and substances.

One of the greatest promises of quantum computers in chemistry is their ability to precisely simulate molecules and their reactions. Classical computers already reach their limits when simulating relatively small molecules, as the complexity of the calculations grows exponentially with the size of the molecule. However, quantum computers can represent the states of molecules in a natural and efficient way, leading to more accurate and actionable insights into their properties and reaction pathways.

Another important area of application is the investigation of catalysts and reaction mechanisms. Quantum computers could help to improve the efficiency of catalysts and discover new catalytic processes by enabling a deeper understanding of reaction pathways and energy barriers. This could lead to more efficient and environmentally friendly production processes in the chemical industry.

Similar to drug development, quantum computers can also be used in chemical research to identify and optimise potential drug candidates. The ability to calculate the binding affinities and stability of drug-target complexes at the quantum level could accelerate the discovery of new drugs and therapies.

Solve optimisation problems

Quantum computers offer promising prospects for solving complex optimisation problems that are difficult to tackle in traditional computational paradigms. Their ability to simultaneously evaluate and optimise a large number of potential solutions makes them ideal for applications in areas such as transport and logistics as well as energy distribution. These systems are typically characterised by high complexity and dynamics, with the search for optimal solutions posing an immense computational challenge. One example of this is the following:

Transport and logistics

In the field of transport and logistics, quantum computers can help to increase the efficiency of supply chains, reduce congestion and optimise transport networks. Optimising such networks requires the consideration of an enormous number of variables, including route planning, vehicle allocation, inventory management and customer requirements. Quantum computers could be able to analyse these variables simultaneously and find optimal or near-optimal solutions in near real-time. This could lead to significant cost savings, improved customer service and a reduction in environmental impact.

A specific example would be the optimisation of routes for delivery vehicles to minimise the number of kilometres driven while ensuring that all deliveries are made on time. By reducing the overall journey time and fuel consumption, not only could operating costs be lowered, but CO_2 emissions could also be reduced.

Energy distribution

In energy distribution, grid operators are faced with the challenge of balancing supply and demand in real time while ensuring the reliability of the grid. With the increasing share of renewable energy sources, which are often volatile and geographically distributed, this task is becoming even more complex. Quantum computers could make a decisive contribution here by solving complex optimisation problems associated with the distribution of energy resources.

One use case could be optimising the flow of energy in a smart grid to maximise efficiency and minimise energy losses. By taking into account factors such as energy generation from different sources, consumption forecasts, storage options and weather conditions, quantum computers could help to optimise energy distribution and improve the use of storage systems and the integration of renewable energies.

Cryptography and security

Quantum computers and their impact on cryptography and security are double-edged. On the one hand, they offer the possibility of developing extremely secure communication methods through quantum encryption. On the other hand, they pose a serious threat to the security of existing encryption methods. This dynamic is central to understanding the future landscape of information security.

Quantum encryption

Quantum encryption, specifically Quantum Key Distribution (QKD), is an advanced approach to secure communication that utilises the principles of quantum mechanics. QKD allows two parties to generate and exchange a secure key without it being intercepted by a third party without being detected. The security of QKD is based on the quantum mechanical principle that measuring a quantum state inevitably changes that state. An eavesdropper attempting to intercept the key would therefore change the quantum information and thus reveal its presence. QKD systems are already under development and offer a potentially unbreakable method of encryption that is suitable for security-critical applications such as government communications, military communications and the transmission of sensitive information in the financial sector.

Threats to existing encryption methods

The ability of quantum computers to solve certain mathematical problems exponentially faster than classical computers poses a serious threat to the security of many currently used encryption standards. In particular, asymmetric cryptosystems such as RSA and ECC (Elliptic Curve Cryptography), which are based on the difficulty of problems such as the factorisation of large numbers or the discrete logarithm in elliptic curves, could be effectively broken by quantum computers. The Shor algorithm, a quantum algorithm that can solve these types of problems in polynomial time, shows the potential scale of the threat. This means that information that is considered securely encrypted today could be decrypted in the future through the development of powerful quantum computers.

The potential threat posed by quantum computers has led to the development of post-quantum cryptography (PQC), a field of research concerned with developing encryption methods that are secure even in the era of quantum computing. PQC methods are based on mathematical problems that are also considered difficult for quantum computers. The research and standardisation of PQC algorithms is currently being intensively pursued in order to enable a seamless transition to more secure encryption methods before powerful quantum computers become generally available.

Finance

Quantum computers offer promising applications in finance, particularly in the areas of risk analysis and portfolio optimisation. This technology has the potential to fundamentally change the way financial institutions perform complex calculations and make decisions by enabling calculations with a speed and complexity that cannot be achieved with conventional computers.

Risk analysis

Risk analysis is a critical component of financial management that aims to assess the extent and probability of financial losses. In modern finance, complex models and simulations, such as Monte Carlo simulations, are used to analyse the distribution of possible future outcomes based on a variety of input parameters. Quantum computers can significantly speed up these simulations by utilising the ability to track a large number of computational paths simultaneously. This could enable financial institutions to perform more accurate risk assessments in less time, which can be invaluable, especially when assessing counterparty risk, market risk and credit risk.

Portfolio optimisation

Portfolio optimisation is the process of selecting the best mix of assets with the aim of minimising risk and/or maximising the expected return, taking into account various constraints (such as budget, risk tolerance, investment horizon). This problem can become mathematically very complex, especially when a large number of assets with complex relationships and uncertainties regarding their expected returns and risks are involved. Quantum computers have the potential to solve these optimisation problems more efficiently by using algorithms that are able to sift through the enormous solution landscape much faster than would be possible with classical optimisation methods. This could lead to better, more information-rich investment strategies that increase returns and minimise risk for investors.

The application of quantum computing in finance is still in its infancy and there are both technical and practical challenges to overcome. These include the development and scaling of quantum hardware, the customisation and creation of specific algorithms for financial applications and issues of data integrity and security. Nevertheless, many financial institutions and technology companies are already working on research projects and pilot programmes to explore the potential of quantum computing in this area.

The future of quantum computers n

Developments in the field of quantum computing technology influence numerous aspects of science, technology, industry and social and ethical norms. These dynamics are reflected in theoretical and technical advances, impacts on science and technology, commercialisation and industrial applications, societal and ethical considerations, challenges and solutions. We will only briefly summarise these considerations here.

Development of topology qubits

Topological qubits are considered a promising way to realise stable quantum computers. These qubits are based on topological states of matter that are naturally resistant to many types of perturbations. Their development could reduce the need for extensive quantum error correction and at the same time extend the coherence times of the qubits, which is an essential prerequisite for practical quantum computers.

Progress in quantum error correction

Quantum error correction is crucial for the realisation of reliable quantum computations. Current advances aim to develop efficient codes and protocols that can address and correct the vulnerability of quantum systems to errors without destroying quantum information. These efforts are crucial for building scalable and practical quantum computers.

Revolution in data processing

Quantum computers promise to revolutionise data processing through their ability to solve problems exponentially faster than classical computers. This could have a transformative impact, particularly in solving problems that require enormous computing power, such as cryptography, materials science and optimisation problems.

New fields of research through quantum simulations

Quantum simulations enable the investigation of phenomena that cannot be simulated using conventional computers. This opens up new fields of research in physics, chemistry and biology and provides insights into complex systems that can expand our understanding of fundamental laws of nature and lead to the development of new technologies.

Commercialisation and industrial applications

The ongoing commercialisation of quantum computing technologies through the development of cloud-based services and platforms is an inevitable trend that is transforming the landscape of quantum computing usage. These platforms enable companies and research organisations to perform quantum computations without having to invest in expensive and complex quantum computing infrastructures themselves. This significantly expands access to quantum computers and facilitates the integration of quantum technologies into existing IT systems.

Making quantum computing available via the cloud democratises access to this advanced technology by enabling small and medium-sized enterprises and researchers worldwide to work at the forefront of quantum research and application. This development not only lowers the barriers to entry for the use of quantum computing, but also promotes wider acceptance and application of quantum technologies in various industries and research fields.

Cloud-based quantum computing services provide a flexible and scalable environment for performing quantum computations, which is particularly important for applications that require variable computing power. Users can scale their projects efficiently, benefiting from the cost advantages and reduced complexity provided by the cloud. In addition, these services accelerate research and development in fields that can benefit from quantum computing technology, such as materials science, pharmaceutical research and complex optimisation problems.

However, the integration of quantum computing technologies into existing IT infrastructures poses a challenge. Cloud platforms bridge this gap by providing interfaces and development tools that facilitate the implementation of quantum algorithms into traditional computing environments. These tools are critical to creating a smooth transition from classical to quantum computing resources and allow developers to take advantage of quantum computing without having to be experts in the field.

Despite the promising benefits, the commercialisation and widespread application of quantum computers face several challenges, including the complexity of quantum algorithms, security concerns and technical limitations of current quantum computers. The development and understanding of quantum algorithms requires specialised knowledge, which is currently limited. In addition, the potential threat posed by quantum computers to existing encryption standards requires a revision of security strategies.

Despite these challenges, continued advances in research and development and collaboration between academia and industry are driving the overcoming of these barriers. The increasing availability of quantum computing resources and the further development of technologies and algorithms suggest that quantum computers will play an important role in many application areas in the near future, making them an integral part of the global IT infrastructure.

Co-operation between science and industry

The growing collaboration between academic institutions and industry plays a central role in promoting the development and application of quantum technologies. These collaborations are a key factor in bridging the gap between theoretical research and practical application, and they have an impact on accelerating the commercialisation of quantum computing technologies.

By combining expertise, resources and interests, these partnerships enable a more efficient transfer of knowledge and technologies from the laboratory to the market. They not only facilitate industry's access to the latest scientific findings and innovations, but also offer academic researchers the opportunity to understand the practical applications and challenges of their work.

These synergies are particularly important in a field as complex and specialised as quantum computing, where technology development cycles are fast and the demands on expertise and infrastructure are high. Companies benefit from the advanced research and talent in universities, while the academic world gains valuable insights into real-world use cases and additional sources of funding through industry partnerships.

The collaboration ranges from joint research projects and prototype development to educational programmes aimed at training a new generation of scientists and engineers to work in quantum technology. In addition, these partnerships play an important role in the formulation of standards and protocols for quantum technologies, which is essential for the creation of an interoperable and secure quantum ecosystem.

Ultimately, such collaborations are helping to shape the commercial landscape for quantum technologies by driving innovation, expanding application areas and helping to create a market that supports the commercial utilisation of quantum computing. This dynamic interaction between academia and industry is critical to unlocking the full potential of quantum technologies and realising their transformative impact on various industries.

Data protection and security

With the advent of quantum computers, the security of digital systems and the protection of sensitive data is facing an unprecedented challenge. These powerful machines have the potential to crack the encryption methods that currently secure most of our digital communications and data storage. This creates an urgent need to re-evaluate and adapt data protection and security strategies. In this context, the development of post-quantum cryptography is proving to be crucial. This new generation of cryptography aims to create algorithms that can ensure the confidentiality and integrity of digital information even in the era of powerful quantum computers.

Post-quantum cryptography represents a proactive approach to address the upcoming security challenges by utilising mathematical problems that are considered hard to solve even for quantum computers. The work on such cryptographic systems is complex and requires a deep understanding of both quantum computing technology and theoretical computer science. Their successful implementation will not only ensure the protection of government and financial communications, but also the security of the everyday digital interactions of billions of users around the world.

This transition to post-quantum cryptography represents an enormous collaborative effort involving scientists, technology companies and regulators to develop and implement standards that will secure digital progress while increasing the level of data protection. The development and deployment of these new cryptographic systems will take time, so it is critical that these efforts are vigorously pursued now. This may ensure that the digital world is prepared for the arrival of quantum computing technology and that the security and confidentiality of information is maintained in this new era.

Education and the labour market

The rapid development of quantum technology will have a profound impact on the labour market by placing new demands on the skills and qualifications of the workforce. In this dynamic environment, the importance of education and training in quantum computing and related disciplines is becoming increasingly clear. In order to be prepared for the coming changes, it is essential that educational institutions and training programmes adapt and expand to meet the future demand for qualified professionals.

113

The promotion of such education does not only start with specialised university programmes, but also requires the integration of basic knowledge about quantum technologies at earlier educational levels. This creates a solid foundation and stimulates interest in these promising fields. Further, continuing education for those already in the workforce is critical to allow the current labour force to develop and retrain in this rapidly evolving field.

The impact of quantum technology on the labour market presents both challenges and opportunities. On the one hand, the change requires proactive adaptation of education systems and the development of new curricula and training programmes. On the other hand, it opens up the possibility for the emergence of new professional fields and career paths that have the potential to change the way we think about work and technological innovation.

Close co-operation between educational institutions, industry and government agencies will be crucial to ensure that the population is prepared for the quantum era. Through targeted investment in education and training, we can create a workforce that is not only prepared for the technological changes, but also actively involved in shaping them. In this way, the transition to quantum technology can be seen not only as a technical challenge, but also as an opportunity for growth and innovation.

Overcoming technical barriers

The realisation of powerful quantum computers presents science and technology with considerable challenges that can only be overcome through ongoing research and development. One of the main hurdles is the susceptibility of quantum systems to errors. Quantum bits, or qubits, are extremely sensitive to external influences, which can lead to errors in quantum computations. The development of effective error correction mechanisms is therefore crucial to ensure reliable and accurate quantum computations.

In addition to error correction, the scaling of quantum computers is a technical barrier. The ability to manage and efficiently interconnect a larger number of qubits is crucial for increasing the computing power of quantum computers. This requires innovative approaches in the physical design of quantum computers as well as in the development of technologies that enable stable and coherent quantum entanglement over larger systems.

Another critical aspect is system integration, i.e. the incorporation of quantum computers into existing IT infrastructures. Seamless integration requires not only the development of compatible interfaces and protocols, but also the adaptation of existing software and networks in order to fully utilise the unique possibilities and requirements of quantum computing.

Overcoming these technical challenges requires a multidisciplinary effort that brings together expertise from physics, computer science, materials science and engineering. Research institutions, universities and industry must work closely together to advance basic research and develop practical solutions for the design and operation of quantum computers.

Despite the complexity and difficulties associated with the development of quantum computers, the potential benefits provide a strong incentive to tackle these challenges. By continuously improving technologies and methods, we are gradually moving towards the goal of realising powerful quantum computers that have the potential to redefine the boundaries of computing and enable advances in numerous scientific and industrial fields.

Development of standards and protocols

The broad application of quantum technologies in various industrial and scientific fields requires the development of uniform standards and protocols. These standards are crucial to ensure smooth compatibility between quantum technologies and existing digital systems, minimise security risks and ensure high reliability of the technology in a wide range of applications.

The creation of such standards requires a coordinated effort that goes beyond individual research groups and companies and involves the global community of scientists, engineers, industry experts and regulators. This collaboration is necessary to develop a common language and common practices that will form the basis for the interoperability of quantum technologies.

The development of standards includes not only technical aspects such as the definition of interfaces, data formats and communication protocols, but also security guidelines that ensure the protection of data in quantum networks and when using quantum computing services. Given the potential ability of quantum computers to compromise existing encryption methods, the introduction of post-quantum cryptography standards is a critical part of these security considerations.

Reliability is another key element addressed by standards. For the use of quantum technologies in critical applications, such as in medicine, finance or logistics, it is essential that systems deliver predictable performance and are robust against errors. Standards in error correction and system diagnostics are therefore of great importance.

The development and implementation of standards in quantum technology is of course still in its infancy, just like the technology itself, but their importance will increase as these technologies continue to mature. Harmonised standards will not only drive technological development and the commercial use of quantum technologies, but will also help to increase user confidence in this new technology.

Promotion of education and skilled labour development

Investment in education and skills development is fundamental to building a robust ecosystem that drives the research, development and commercial application of quantum technologies. Such an ecosystem will allow the enormous potential offered by quantum technologies to be fully realised, while ensuring that society as a whole can benefit from the associated advances.

Creating a solid educational foundation in quantum physics, quantum computing and related disciplines is the first step in educating a new generation of scientists, engineers and technicians who are familiar with the complex challenges and opportunities of these technologies. This requires a revision of curricula at different levels of education to provide basic knowledge of quantum technologies and to stimulate interest and understanding in this field.

In addition, specialised training programmes and certifications for professionals already in the workforce are crucial to enhance existing skills and adapt them to the specific requirements of quantum technology. Such programmes help to bridge the gap between traditional technologies and the new quantum technologies and enable professionals to continuously develop and keep pace with the rapid advances in this field.

In addition to specialised training, the promotion of interdisciplinary skills is important, as the application of quantum technologies often requires collaboration across disciplinary boundaries. Knowledge of computer science, mathematics, materials science and other relevant fields is essential to effectively solve the complex problems associated with the development and implementation of quantum technologies.

Investment in education and skills development is also crucial to promote the commercial use of quantum technologies. A well-educated talent pool is a prerequisite for the creation and growth of start-ups and companies that develop, apply and commercialise quantum technologies. This in turn helps to create jobs, strengthen the economy and secure technological leadership in this fast-growing field.

Ultimately, investments in education and skills development are not only investments in individual career development, but also in the social and economic future. A strong ecosystem that supports the research, development and application of quantum technologies is essential to realise the many benefits that these technologies offer and to remain competitive on a global level.

Conclusion

Overall, quantum computing technology is on the cusp of profound changes in many areas. Successfully overcoming the technical and social challenges will be crucial to realising the full potential of this technology and achieving positive effects on science, technology, the economy and society.

Predicting a specific date for a breakthrough in quantum computing remains a challenge, as it depends on a variety of rapidly evolving technological, scientific and financial factors. While there has been significant progress in quantum computing technology in recent years, a decisive breakthrough that would make quantum computers superior for a wide range of applications has yet to materialise.

The development and improvement of qubits, which are the basic units of quantum computers, as well as advances in quantum error correction, are major technical challenges that still need to be overcome. Solving these problems is crucial for the creation of practical quantum computers capable of performing complex calculations that go far beyond the capabilities of today's classical computers.

Quantum computing research is benefiting from increasing investment from both the public and private sectors, which is accelerating the development of this technology. This financial support underlines the confidence in the potential of quantum computing to bring about transformative change in various fields such as materials science, pharmaceuticals and complex optimisation problems.

Although some companies have already announced the achievement of so-called quantum superiority for specific tasks, the general application of quantum computers that outperform classical computers in all areas is still a long way off. Experts are cautiously optimistic that significant breakthroughs in quantum computing are possible within the next decade in specialised applications, but a comprehensive breakthrough that makes quantum computing generally applicable could still be two decades or more away.

However, the dynamics of progress in quantum computing are difficult to predict and unexpected scientific breakthroughs could accelerate development timelines. Continued research and development in this area is crucial to overcoming existing challenges and realising the full potential of quantum technology.

The future of quantum computing therefore remains an exciting field whose timeline is flexible and adaptable to new discoveries and technological advances, but which defies concrete prediction.